I was BORN to Win

How to
*Think it, Say it, Believe it, & **Live** it!*

James A. Smith

IBW Publishing
ibwpublishing.com

I

I Was Born to Win: How to Think It, Say It, Believe It, & Live It!

© Copyright 2008 by James A. Smith. This book was manufactured in the United States of America. All rights reserved. No part of it may be reproduced in any form or by any electronic or mechanical means including information storage and retrieval systems without permission in writing from the publishers, except a reviewer, who may quote brief passages in a review. Published by IBW Publishing, Bradenton, FL. 34202. (877) U CAN WIN (822.6946) www.ibwpublishing.com.

To receive a free biweekly newsletter containing personal development techniques, inspiring stories, and upcoming events please go to www.iwasborntowin.com/subscribe.

Limit of Liability/Disclaimer - Although the author and publisher have exhaustively researched all sources to ensure the accuracy and completeness of the information contained in this book, neither James A. Smith or IBW Publishing assume any responsibility for errors, inaccuracies, omissions, or any other inconsistency herein. Any perceived slights against people or organizations are certainly unintentional.

Colleges, universities, churches, corporations, and trainers. Quantity discounts are available on bulk purchases of this book for educational training purposes, fundraising, or gift-giving. Special books, booklets, or excerpts can also be created to fit your needs. For more information, contact the marketing department on line at www.iwasborntowin.com or call 877 U CAN WIN (877.822.6946)

Edited by: Velvet Torres, Amy Merrill, John Gregory, and MariLynn Polachek

Cover design by Sarah Lipp, sarah@adsgainc.com

Cover creation by Mark Spatz, mspatz@emarketg.com

Logo created by Lee Ann Martin, leeann@lamartindesign.com

Scripture taken from the HOLY BIBLE, NEW INTERNATIONAL VERSION®. Copyright © 1973, 1978, 1984 International Bible Society. Used by permission of Zondervan. All rights reserved.

The "NIV" and "New International Version" trademarks are registered in the United States Patent and Trademark Office by International Bible Society. Use of either trademark requires the permission of International Bible Society.

Library of Congress Control Number: 2008920310

ISBN: 978-0-615-18346-6   First Edition

1. Self-Help: Motivational & Inspirational
2. Self-Help: Personal Growth – Success
3. Self-Help: Spiritual

Dedication

This book is dedicated to the two most important women in my life. My mother, Cathy Carr, and my daughter, Cassandra Rose Smith, whom I call "Boogie."

Momma, your determination and persistence have always been admirable. Thank you for your willingness to help anyone, any way, anytime. I love you for all that you do.

Boogie, I am honored that God gave me the privilege and responsibility of being your Dad. Thank you so much for patiently listening, and even helping, with my lectures, ideas, visions, and speeches. I will always be your number one cheerleader. I love you immensely.

About the Author

James A. Smith brings over 20 years experience from the fields of direct sales, marketing, leadership, and motivation. In addition to speaking and writing, James hosts a weekly *I Was Born to Win* radio show, delivering encouragement and techniques for personal growth and development. He stimulates audiences with his charismatic style, humorous insights, and contagious high energy. Inspiring, passionate, optimistic, and encouraging are words frequently used to describe James. His unique personality allows him to effectively communicate through hope, humor, and harmony.

From humble beginnings in the small southern town of Plant City, Florida, James now devotes his life to cheering for others, especially the perceived underdog. In 2005 James diverted much of his focus from a successful career in the mortgage industry to join the world renowned Zig Ziglar team in Dallas, TX as an outside independent speaker and trainer. James left Ziglar in 2006 and currently serves people through speaking, seminars, workshops, consulting, and radio.

Personally, James leads two weekly, Christian based, adult singles events that focus on social and personal development. He is an ALL PRO DADS® team captain and father of one daughter - Cassandra Smith. James resides in Bradenton, Florida.

Book Reviews

"If you embrace the philosophy that 'you never graduate from learning' then you'll embrace James A. Smith's book *I Was Born to Win!* By applying James' principles on growing from the inside and giving from the inside, you will learn how to live life to the fullest! His chapter on *Pain for the Proper Purpose is Productive* is a must read for any of us who face life's challenges." - **Bryan Flanagan, Dallas, TX. Director of Training, Zig Ziglar Corporation and author of** *Now go Sell Somebody Something!*

"I don't know anyone more passionate about life than James A. Smith. He has an awesome desire to help others live up to their full potential. I appreciate his encouraging spirit and his dedication to personal growth. He's a Winner!" - **Dr. Tim Passmore, Pastor of Woodland – The Community Church in Bradenton, Florida and author of** *OUTCOME: A Blueprint for Becoming an Effective Church* **and** *One Fry Short: A Journey Toward Self Discovery and Emotional Success.*

"It was a pleasure to have the opportunity to read *I Was Born to Win*. Knowing James personally, this book is an accurate portrayal of his philosophy of life, his plan for success and his spiritual outlook. It made me think, reflect, laugh and cry. The ideas, concepts and suggestions could be life changing. I would recommend it to anyone experiencing the journey of life." - **Gary Salyers, Bradenton, FL.**

"Thanks for your work on writing a book that clearly defines what true success looks like as well as offering understandable strategies for achieving it. After reading it I am certain of two things. First, that it will benefit all who take the time to read it and second, if it was written by one of today's more recognized authors it would quickly move up the best seller list. Thanks for encouraging all of us to go out and 'knock'em alive'." - **Chip Powell, Bradenton, FL.**

"I approached the reading of the book with a large dose of skepticism as the whole concept seemed to be just another self-help book based on everyone reaching their highest potential as humans. The book is so much more than that! It connects the reader to the only source available for a life of meaning, relevance and joy. It is well written and enjoyable to read while being profound in its message of God being the power of everyone who is truly a 'winner'." – **Billy Tullos, Bradenton, FL.**

Table of Contents

About the Author IV
Book Reviews V

Part I: Winning 13

Winning vs. Losing 15

Chapter 1 Is This Winning 19
He Had it All 19
He Broke it All 19
Do We Want it All 21
The Wishlist 22
The Rest of the Story 22
The End of the Stories 24

Chapter 2 The Ultimate Human Motive 27
Sign by the X 27
What's Love got to do with It 29
The Power of Love 30
The Way of Love 31
The Real Thing 32

Chapter 3 Winning at Life 35
Motives and Expectations 35
Risk and Expectations 36
Winning Defined 39
The Cycle of Life 40
How Do We Win More 42

Part II: I Grow From the Inside 43

Chapter 4 Inner Growth 45
Who Needs Me 45
Are You Running on E – Ego 46
Self-maintenance or Selfish 47
The Gas Chamber 47
Don't Hit the Cone 49

Chapter 5 Self-Image ... 53
See a Winner ... 53
In the Beginning ... 55
Failure is an Event, Not a Person ... 56
Comparing ... 57
The CEO and the Seed ... 59
What Did You Say ... 61
Self-Talk ... 62

Chapter 6 Conceive, Believe, Achieve ... 65
Conceive ... 65
Believe ... 66
Achieve ... 67
Change the Input ... 68

Chapter 7 Forgiveness ... 69
Would You Forgive Him ... 69
Detoxification ... 70
Humility ... 71
Release the Grudge ... 72
Forgive Ourselves ... 72
Quack, Quack ... 73

Part III: I Give on the Outside ... 77

Chapter 8 The Value of Giving ... 79
Doing Good and Feeling Better ... 79
Service Learning ... 81
The Helpers' High ... 82
Outside the Hospital Window ... 82
Prevent Defense ... 84
Making a Difference ... 85

Chapter 9 Paradigm Shifts ... 87
The Difference between You and Me ... 87
Excuse Me, May I Help You ... 88
Please Hear What I'm *Not* Saying ... 89
Father's Day with Daddy ... 91

Chapter 10 Personality and Behavior 95
- Determining Styles 96
- What Style are You 97
- Different Personality Styles 98
- Personality Patterns 101
- Overusing a Strength 101
- Out of Balance 102
- Balancing Our Strengths 103

Chapter 11 Applying Personality 105
- When Parenting 105
- In Relationships 105
- How to Recognize 106
- Communicating in Style 106
- What Turns You Off 107
- What Motivates You 108
- Camping in Style 110

Chapter 12 Winning - On Purpose 113
- What Good Am I 114
- The Purpose of Life 114
- Filling the Needs of Others 115
- The Wrong Place at the Right Time 116
- The Elite 20% 117
- Looking for Your Purpose 118

Part IV: I Gain From My Pain 123

Chapter 13 Purpose, Problems, and Pain 125
- Fighting on Behalf of Children 126
- They Saved Each Others Life 127
- Through Their Pain 129
- Passion from Pain 129
- Passion after the Pain 130

Chapter 14 Pain for the Proper Purpose is Productive 133

Pain for the Proper Purpose is Productive 133
Why Does God Allow Pain in Our Life 134
Failing is Part of Winning 137
Good Pain vs. Bad Pain 138
Pain is Part of the Process 138
Pain Promotes Positive Performance 139

Chapter 15 Fear 141

The Fear of Fear 142
Empire State Building 143
Fear vs. Winning 144
Fear Distorts Our Focus 144
Align Focus with Desires 145

Part V: I Gauge My Growing, Giving, and Gaining..149

Chapter 16 Goals 151

Do I Have a Deal for You 151
Testing Your Aim 152
Roadmap for the Winner's Highway 153
The Day Before Vacation 153
What is a Goals System 154
Why Have a Goals System 154

Chapter 17 The Goals Process 157

Balance 157
Step 1. Make a List 158
Step 2. Identify Final Goal 159
Step 3. Qualification 160
Step 4. Benefits 163
Step 5. Specify 163
Step 6. Small Steps 164
Step 7. Possible Obstacles 164
Step 8. Action List 165
Step 9. Commitment 167
Step 10. Notes/tracking 167

Chapter 18 A System for Action 169
Fast Food Systems 169
What He Stands For.. 169
Slow Down to Speed Up 170
Automatic Actions 171
Conscious and Subconscious 172

Chapter 19 Tracking and Gauging 175
Tracking - Strengths and Habits 176
Identify another's Primary Personality 177
Familiarize Yourself with Individual Strengths 177
Learn Specific Areas Where Others Need You 178
Creating Positive Habits 179
Summarized Outline of chapters 1-19 181

Part VI: A Spiritual Experience 183

Chapter 20 Dying a Winner 185
Painting the Picture.. 185
False Perceptions 187
The Oxygen of Life 189
Faith or Facts 190
The Owner's Manual 191
Eternal Love 193
Eternal Security 195
The Power of Perfect Love 197
Acknowledgements.. 201
Footnotes/References.. 203

Part I: Winning

Winning vs. Losing

I _____ was born to win!
(Your name here)

Winning is for losers. If you have ever been called a loser or felt like a loser, you're a prime candidate for winning! To confirm such a statement, I ask you to let your mind ponder. Imagine, for a moment, that you win at everything you try. You consistently come in first place, complete everything you start, obtain exactly what you desire, and always get your way. You are simply the *cat's meow*.

Now, imagine you always lose at everything. You always finish last - if you finish at all. You never achieve anything. If it was raining money you would get hit in the head by a bill collector. Nothing ever goes your way.

If you were given the choice between always winning and always losing, I think it's fair to say you would pick the *always win* route. After all, typically, winning is pleasurable and losing is painful. However, if we were *always* winning, it could not be pleasurable. Why? Winning is only valuable because of losing. Ironically, losing is necessary in order to win. It's the pain from losing that makes the pleasure from winning so desirable. Just like hot and cold, how could we ever know the value of being warm if we have never been cold? If you've never lost, you will not qualify as a good candidate for appreciating the joy of winning. Have you ever lost at anything? I certainly have and once I realized this, I knew I was *very* qualified to enjoy winning and so are you!

Who are some of your favorite winners in life? Are any of them sports figures? How about a Hollywood star, a singer, teacher, preacher, president, friend, or parent? If you could be one of them, who would you be? Seriously, if you could be anyone in life, who would it be? Do you have a specific name in mind? Why would you want to be that person? Will you write down your answers so we can refer back to them?

I would be _____

because _____

Here are a few other questions to think about.

- If winning is so wonderful, why aren't there more winners in life?
- Do you believe it's easier to win or to lose?
- Why hasn't anyone written a book that teaches us how to lose at life?

I have never heard of anyone signing up for a course on advanced lying, selfishness, or hatred. I've never heard of a social group or network called the *losers* club. Whenever I speak on this subject, I ask the audience, *is there anyone here who wants to be a loser today?* So far, I've never seen a hand raised. There is simply no market for people who *want* to lose. Then I ask you again, why are there not more winners in life?

I asked you earlier to choose one person in the whole world that you would want to be if given the choice. Out of the six billion people on earth today, who is that particular one that is so special? I hope the lucky winner that won your heart, above all the others, is...*you!* Unfortunately, many people will choose someone besides themselves. There was a time I would have made many other choices besides myself. It is very difficult to consistently win in life until we accept ourselves. *You* are qualified, right now, to be that special winner you were born to be. The opinion you have of yourself has more influence on you than any other opinion in this world. In addition, the opinion you have of yourself determines how you will be influenced by the opinions of others.

Regardless of where you are in your journey through life, you will discover more of your inner winner, not when you complete this book, but as you read it. Not because of the book - because of you. The information in this book is simply a tool. Like any other tool, it will produce according to how the craftsman (you, the reader) uses and applies it.

Here are just a few things you can expect in this book. You will be challenged and motivated by seeing different views of yourself and your desires. You will learn about different personality types and why you do the things you do. You will identify and build upon your unique strengths. We will discuss what it means to have a specific purpose in life and ways to identify or confirm yours. You will learn the positive sides to both fear and pain. You will discover why only three percent of the population has a goals system and if it's worth it. You will learn a powerful and effective system for replacing bad habits with good ones. You will feel more empowered and hopeful.

I, personally, have been a student of what you're about to read. It has made a profound difference in my life. I've always been pretty good at avoiding most troubles in life, except...*temptation!* As a matter of fact, the only thing I've ever been addicted to is...*more*. Perhaps you know someone like this. All joking aside, it was only a few years ago when I struggled with many destructive addictions (I cover them in more detail later). I didn't like myself or who I had become. I didn't like where I had been or where I was headed. Today, I am completely free from all of those addictions and poisons! More importantly, I am free from the poor self-image I had of myself. As you might expect, I am more excited about life than I've ever been. Or, as we say back home, I'm happier than a thrown back catfish!

While all of the following are very helpful and needed, I have never received treatment from Alcoholics Anonymous (A.A.), a counselor, therapist, preacher, psychologist, or psychiatrist. I have never been prescribed nor taken any type of medication to assist or treat any of my struggles. The treatment plan that worked for me is outlined in this book. Maybe you've never struggled with a specific addiction. Maybe there are just a few areas of your life that you would like to improve upon. Maybe you're just looking for ideas. This is not a "one size fits all" plan. It has the flexibility to offer insight on areas that are specific to your life. You will certainly be familiar with some of the information. Chances are great you will enjoy a lot of it and might even disagree with some of it. But if you're positively changed by any of it, then both of us will be able to say and validate with a little more assurance, *I was born to win!*

This book consists of six different parts. In the first part, I will share different perceptions of winning. We will then establish an applicable definition for winning and how it fits into your life. In parts two through five, I will cover the specific steps of *how* to win. Here are those four steps in a first person, present tense, positive affirmation. It is my goal that you will say them to yourself often.

- **I grow from the inside**
- **I give on the outside**
- **I gain from my pain**
- **I gauge my growing, giving, and gaining**

In the last part, I share my personal spiritual experience and how it relates to winning. It's the very experience which motivated me to write this book.

I've shared my heart with you throughout this book. I hope you will do the same with me. Please give your input as often as you feel prompted at www.iwasborntowin.com/readerinput.

Chapter 1
Is This Winning

Whoever is winning at the moment will always seem to be invincible.

— George Orwell, British Author

He Had it All

In the 1920's there was a man, 19 years of age, who received a multi-million dollar inheritance which he ultimately turned into billions. He was a mastermind, an oil tycoon, a movie producer, an aviator, and one of the richest men in the world. He owned studios, hotels, restaurant chains, TWA airlines, and several other companies. He built the largest and fastest airplanes. He broke world records in flying distances and speeds. He also received several awards for producing movies. He wanted for nothing. If something wasn't available to his liking, he would buy the company that was capable of providing it. If he wanted you to work for him badly enough, he would hire you on the spot and often times pay double what you were already earning. He had many beautiful women on his arm, including several Hollywood actresses. In 1953 he launched a medical institution bearing his name. With an endowment of over $16 billion, the *Howard Hughes Medical Center*[1] is the largest of its kind devoted to biological and medical research.

He Broke it All

Another well known man broke more achievement records, even after his death, than most will ever break in a lifetime! Born in 1935, in a two-room house in Tupelo, Mississippi, he came from humble beginnings. He mixed gospel singing with rhythm and blues. His style of music and dance broke racial barriers and he was an international phenomenon by the age of 21. Elvis Presley, in addition to his enormous musical career, also starred in 33 successful movies.

Musically, he globally sold over one billion records, more than any other artist in history. He won 178 combined gold, platinum, or multi-platinum awards for albums and singles. The closest anyone else has ever come to those winnings are the Beatles, with 114. Elvis was named one of the Ten Outstanding Young Men in the Nation for 1970 by the U.S. Jaycees. His talent, good looks, charisma, humor, and humility attracted millions to him. In January of 1973, he made television history with a worldwide audience viewing his *Aloha from Hawaii* performance. The show didn't air on TV in the continental U.S. until that April and attracted 51% of the viewing audience. It was reportedly seen by more American households than man's first walk on the moon.

In 1977, the funeral of Elvis was attended by hundreds of thousands of fans. He's been on stamps all over the world since his US postage stamp was introduced in 1993. To date it's the highest selling stamp in US History with over 124 million. He is arguably the most impersonated person on the planet. The demand, even today, is so high that some radio stations exclusively present Elvis impersonation material. There are even cult followers who impersonate him and believe they are called by "The King" to finish his work. Airlines have offered discounts on his celebrated holidays. Universities teach about him. There are festivals, events, and contests celebrating him and his impersonators. Fortune magazine named him the top deceased income earner for five straight years (2000–2005) grossing $45 million in 2005 alone, 28 years after his death! His mansion and estate, Graceland, is the second most visited residence today - second only to the White House. In 2002, despite the heavy rain, an estimated 40,000 people attended Graceland for the 25th anniversary of his death. That's more than attend some NFL football games.

Hughes and Elvis were huge icons in their own right, achieving monumental feats. They had an enormous impact on society and our culture that continues to this day.

Chapter 1: Is This Winning

Do We Want it All

How would you like to have it all like Hughes or break all the records like Elvis? What do you <u>really want</u> out of life? What <u>motivates you</u>? What is <u>your definition of a winner</u> in relation to life? Isn't it true most of us claim we don't need what Hughes and Elvis had; the cars, mansions, fame, money, power, and all kinds of other stuff? Our actions, however, often indicate the opposite. It's obvious that many of us believe this *stuff* will make us happy. Sure, we may attempt to show a deeper side. One that says we are not materialistic or shallow. The reality is, to a degree our perception of winning is typically achieving and obtaining tangible items, positions, or status. Remember when I asked you which winner you would be in life if you could choose anyone? Then I asked you why? What was your answer to the second question, the *why*? Was it because of some *thing* they possessed?

The more we count on obtaining a *thing* in order to win, the more we head toward losing. If it takes a materialistic item to make us or break us, it will usually break us. Our own perception of winning must line up with the reality of winning.

> "If it takes a materialistic item to make us or break us, it will usually break us"

You've probably heard it said before - *perception is reality*. <u>Whatever we believe</u> winning to be, <u>that</u>, <u>we will chase</u>. Therefore, it's vitally important we have the proper perspective.

The Wishlist

When people are asked for their definition of winning in life, several different views and opinions are expressed. Overall, most people relate winning to what I call the *wishlist*™. Most of us want:

Wellness – a healthy mind, body, and soul

Information – education, wisdom, and knowledge

Serenity – peace of mind

Hope – for life and the future

Lasting relationships – with substance and meaning

Income – comfortably pay bills, savings

Security – stability and safety

Targets – somewhere to aim, a purpose

I certainly want the *wishlist*, how about you? Some people want it so badly they will literally do anything to get it - lie, cheat, steal, or even kill. Others enjoy the *wishlist* in full abundance. Its contents seem to be universally acceptable as the answer or tool that will make us a winner. But will it?

The Rest of the Story

I only scratched the surface, earlier, of what Howard Hughes obtained and accomplished before he died in 1976. From the surface, he would have been considered a winner by any type of materialistic measure. However, there is another side to the story.

As a side note, I am reminded of the little boy who was out walking his dog. It was a short, fat, stubby, yellow - sickly looking dog, very unattractive to say the least. As they were about to cross the street, the boy noticed a man walking towards them with a beautiful, healthy looking dog. As they got closer, the man suggested the little boy take another route. "Son, my dog is a pit bull with a champion blood line. He does not like other dogs and has already killed five of them this year. Please do not allow your dog to come near him," said the man.

Chapter 1: Is This Winning

"Mr., I'm not too concerned about my dog, you just keep an eye on yours," replied the little boy. As they moved closer, the pit bull started growling and making sounds that would scare most animals. It took every ounce of strength the owner had just to restrain his dog. "Son, please keep your dog away, I am begging you!" cried the man. The little boy insisted that his little dog would be just fine.

As fate would have it, the two dogs locked up and started fighting. Within seconds the little yellow dog took one bite and ripped the bull dog in half, killing it instantly. The owner was obviously surprised and very upset as he stunningly said, "I've never witnessed anything like this before. What kind of dog do you have there son?" To that the boy replied, "Before we chopped his tail off and painted him yellow, he was an alligator!"

Things are not always as they seem. Allegedly, Howard Hughes didn't have many friends but plenty of enemies. He was sued many times – often by his own choice. Even with all of his money, he was tighter than guitar strings. He was constantly trying to get away without paying his fair share of taxes. To beat the competition, he would hire and maintain the best managers by promising them large amounts of bonus money after they left his company. He was able to do this by arranging a scam with the new employee to purposely and publicly criticize them upon their departure of the company. They would then sue Hughes for public defamation and receive money, tax-free. It's reported that one of his employees was rewarded over $2 million. Supposedly, Hughes even started living in hotels to avoid declaring legal residency in any state that would require personal income taxes. It wasn't long before laws were passed stating that anyone living in a state for 180 days was subject to the tax in that state. So, Hughes started moving from state to state just under the 180-day limit.

He suffered from obsessive compulsive behavior, specifically with the fear of catching germs from anything. It got so bad that he locked himself in a separate room and didn't see his second wife for years prior to their divorce. He would eventually become a total recluse and lock himself in a hotel. With the exception of medical aids, he spent the last decade of his life alone. He battled with depression and addictions to codeine, Valium, and other drugs. When he died at the age of 71, the FBI had to fingerprint him to prove identity because he was so unrecognizable. His hair, beard, fingernails, and toenails had grown grossly long. The once 6'4" athletic playboy of Hollywood weighed only ninety pounds when he died. It is alleged that broken off hypodermic needles were still in his body. The medical examiner said cause of death was neglect.

Howard Hughes was worth an estimated $2.5 billion when he died, and that was in 1976. Yet, he died a very miserable man. Ironically, the Hughes Medical Center was started because Howard wanted to understand, according to his own words, *the genesis of life itself.*

The End of the Stories

The end of life for Elvis is more publicly known because of his popularity. He lost interest in doing concerts and looked for other challenges in acting. Unhappy with his career in acting, he went back to touring. Toward the end of Elvis' life he became excessively overweight. Allegedly he would sleep day and night when he wasn't on stage. Elvis became addicted to prescription drugs and ended up dying at the very early age of forty two. The reported cause of death was polypharmacy - the over use of prescription drugs. It is said that fourteen drugs were detected in his system, ten in significant quantities. According to his cousin Billy Smith, Elvis started having phobias about germs, people, and future events. Smith said, on more than one occasion, Elvis reminded him of Howard Hughes.

> "Both of them loved what they obtained but neither one loved what they became."

I must confess, I had never heard of any type of comparison between Hughes and Elvis prior to writing this. I found it quite ironic that both of them loved what they obtained but neither one loved what they became. The stories of Elvis and Howard Hughes are all too common. Both men achieved so much and rose to such heights. Yet, in the end, most of us would decline an opportunity to trade places with either of them. It is very possible that they lacked enough love on the inside to overcome their fears from the outside. Have you ever felt that way? I certainly have.

You and I are no different than either of them in many aspects. All of us are on a constant search for the *wishlist*. We have an inner desire to win more. I am not attempting, in any way, to undermine the lives of Hughes or Elvis. They're simply two iconic figures to whom most of us can relate. It's fair to assume that both of them would have traded everything they ever possessed for a different ending.

Today, unlike any other time, more of the *wishlist* exists than ever before. There is also more depression, loneliness, suicides, and heartache. Thus far, from everything we have covered, I ask you, is this winning? You'll have to answer for yourself, but it's nowhere near winning in my book (no pun intended).

Summary

Points to ponder –

The *wishlist* is a great tool but a pitiful master.

The outside of a person won't always show the inside.

It's not how you start – it is how you finish that matters the most.

What would a winner do?

Love the *wishlist* less and love myself more.

Chapter 2
The Ultimate Human Motive

Whatever touches the nerve of motive, whatever shifts man's moral position, is mightier than steam, or calorie, or lightning

- Edwin Hubbel Chapin, American Author, Clergyman

If we look deep underneath most of the sorrow and pain in life, we will usually expose an interesting motive. People are trying to achieve or obtain those *things* we discussed in the last chapter. There's nothing wrong with trying to achieve or obtain things. However, when we conclude that those things make us a winner we are setting ourselves up for disappointment. In many cases, the more we try to win, the more we lose.

In addition to Hughes and Elvis, there are countless other stories about famous actors, singers, sports figures, pastors, and corporate scandals like Enron. The stories have no prejudice. From the presidents of great countries to our next-door neighbor, the song and tune remain constant. Many of us are trying to win but we end up paying the price in such a losing way. Is winning all it's really cracked up to be? Yes! - provided we have a proper perception of what winning really is.

Sign by the X

Lots of money and time have been spent looking for keys to the winner's formula. Many would sign a contract right now for the true answers. Before you grab your pen, let's leave the surface of life for a moment and dig a little deeper to find out why we really want the *wishlist*.

Part I: Winning

From psychologist Abraham Maslow's popular theory of human needs to other forms of pop psychology, we are told humans desire the following. Beyond the fundamental needs of survival and safety, we want to be needed, wanted, and special. We want to feel important, included, worthy, and accepted. These desires are simply the surface proof of our ultimate inner desire - love. *All* desires, including fundamental, are subordinate to our main desire…love. That's right, true love is what we are trying to find buried within our *wishlist*. I realize it is cliché and easy to simplify the word *love*. I'm certainly not talking about romance, how you love your shoes, or how you love your favorite meal. Perhaps you're rolling your eyes right now because we've heard plenty about love. When I first share this with people, beyond a typical head nod of confirmation, I get one of two responses. Women will smile so wide it looks like they ate a banana sideways! Men will lean back, fold their arms, and look at me like they would rather chew on aluminum.

Unfortunately, the word *love,* aside from *God*, is possibly the most abused, misused, and exaggerated word in our language. It has been so abused, that sadly, many of us associate it with lots of pain, fear, and anger. However, I challenge you to think of the top five, ten, fifty, or hundred things you want out of life. Then ask yourself why you want them. Then continue asking *why* to those answers. Eventually your answers will usually trace right back to…love. When it comes to conscious choices made with a sound mind, love is the ultimate underlying motive.

When I first shared this concept with my daughter, she was 12 years old. She wasn't buying it at all - not even on a payment plan. She finally flipped her cell phone open, rolled her eyes, then closed the flap quickly and said, *"So let me get this straight. You're saying I opened and closed my phone because I want to be loved?"* We certainly laughed. But guess what? If you ask *why*, it will trace right back to love. Why did she open the phone? So she could make a point. Why did she want to make a point? To be validated, valued, significant, or to feel important, smart, and understood. See where I'm headed?

Will you think about this for a moment? The *wishlist*, along with everything we do in life - good or bad, is for the pursuit of this one treasure called love. Am I saying the reason for a criminal's behavior is because they want love? Am I suggesting that children fight because they want love? Am I claiming people are afraid or angry because they want love? Yes, yes, and yes.

I expect you know people who are full of love. They spend more time helping folks rather than hurting them. Regardless of any perceptions we associate with love, the fact is, *true* love is the force that drives you and me to even care about existing. Mahatma Gandhi said "Where there is love there is life." When we consciously grasp this, and then use the ability we already have plus the God-given desire that's *already* inside of us, winning can increase immediately! You then get to enjoy the *wishlist* rather than be enslaved by it. If the *wishlist* has to come before winning, we will lose every time.

What's Love got to do with It

Warren Buffet was interviewed by CNBC in November 2006. Buffet is currently the CEO of Berkshire-Hathaway, an investment firm. At the time of interview, he was the second richest person in the world. People literally pay thousands to learn from him and what he does to make money. In the year 2006, he committed to donate $31 billion dollars of his fortune! It was, at the time, the largest charitable gift in history. Just to put that amount into perspective, $31 billion is 31,000 different piles of one million dollars. If you spent it at the rate of $100,000 per day, it would take you over 849 years to spend what he gave away!

When asked what his secret to success was, Buffet replied, *"When people get to my age (76), and they have the people who love them that they want to love them, they're successful. It doesn't make any difference whether they have $1,000 in the bank or a billion dollars in the bank."* "But you're talking to a CNBC audience, Mr. Buffet. Let's talk about financial and professional success," said the reporter.

"*Success is really doing what you love and doing it well.*" replied Buffet.

The reporter really did an amazing job by probing for a second answer because she knows people have a hard time accepting the whole *love* part as being the answer. Here's a man that has so much money, when he writes a check the bank bounces! Yet, he nails it. When we nail it, excitement arrives in full force.

The Power of Love

Love is the best antidepressant—but many of our ideas about it are wrong. The less love you have, the more depressed you are likely to feel. That statement is a headline from an article in Psychology Today by Ellen McGrath[2]. Here's more of that article.

> *Love is as critical for your mind and body as oxygen. It's not negotiable. The more connected you are, the healthier you will be both physically and emotionally. The less connected you are, the more you are at risk. It is also true that the less love you have, the more depression you are likely to experience in your life. Love is probably the best antidepressant there is because one of the most common sources of depression is feeling unloved. Most depressed people don't love themselves and they do not feel loved by others. They also are very self-focused, making them less attractive to others and depriving them of opportunities to learn the skills of love.*
>
> *There is a mythology in our culture that love just happens. As a result, the depressed often sit around passively waiting for someone to love them. But love doesn't work that way. To get love and keep love you have to go out and be active and learn a variety of specific skills.*
>
> *Most of us get our ideas of love from popular culture. We come to believe that love is something that sweeps us off our feet. But the pop-culture ideal of love consists of unrealistic images created for entertainment, which is one reason so many of us are set up to be depressed. It's a part of our national vulnerability, like eating junk food, constantly stimulated by images of instant gratification. We think it is love when it's simply distraction and infatuation.*

One consequence is that when we hit real love we become upset and disappointed because there are many things that do not fit the cultural ideal. Some of us get demanding and controlling, wanting someone else to do what we think our ideal of romance should be, without realizing our ideal is misplaced. It is not only possible but necessary to change one's approach to love to ward off depression.

She goes on to list strategies that will, according to her, help us *get more of what you want out of life—to love and be loved.*

The Way of Love

Perhaps you've heard at weddings what many have referred to as the greatest love letter of all time.

If I speak in the tongues of men and of angels, but have not love, I am only a resounding gong or a clanging cymbal. If I have the gift of prophecy and can fathom all mysteries and all knowledge, and if I have a faith that can move mountains, but have not love, I am nothing. If I give all I possess to the poor and surrender my body to the flames, but have not love, I gain nothing.

Love is patient, love is kind. It does not envy, it does not boast, it is not proud. It is not rude, it is not self-seeking, it is not easily angered, and it keeps no record of wrongs. Love does not delight in evil but rejoices with the truth. It always protects, always trusts, always hopes, and always perseveres. Love <u>never</u> dies.

That letter was written by the apostle Paul to his family in Corinth almost 2,000 years ago[3]. He goes on to say, *"These three things remain; faith, hope, and love. But the greatest of these is love."*

Also in the Bible in the Song of Solomon, which is referred to as the Song of Songs, meaning the best-of-the-best, it says, *"Love is as strong as death, its jealousy as enduring as the grave. Love flashes like fire, the brightest kind of flame. Many waters cannot quench love, nor can rivers drown it. If a man tried to buy love with all his wealth his offer would be utterly scorned."*[4]

The Real Thing

As already mentioned, love has been abused more than most things. We tend to give so many different things the opportunity to quench our thirst for love. This motivates people to manipulate others by dangling counterfeit love in front of their face. I challenge you to make a copy of Paul's letter and use it as a measuring device. You will quickly find there are many false, phony, and counterfeit versions of the real thing. Insert the five most important things or people in your life and see if they fit.

_____ *is patient,* _____ *is kind. It does not envy, it does not boast, it is not proud. It is not rude, it is not self-seeking, it is not easily angered, and it keeps no record of wrongs.* _____ *does not delight in evil but rejoices with the truth. It always protects, always trusts, always hopes, and always perseveres.* For a short period, alcohol and other drugs were a large part of my life. I can assure you, booze and marijuana are not patient or kind. This is a wonderful tool for helping both you and me eliminate areas that will distract us from enjoying more of life.

I love my daughter dearly and refer to these standards often to assist me in parenting. I am also teaching her to use this same measuring device. Nowhere does it tell her to go against her morals in the name of love. True love doesn't suggest she allow abuse or controlling behavior in relationships with friends or others. As you know, there are many other examples of false love. No wonder it is taken so lightly.

The secret service was established in 1865 for the sole purpose of decreasing counterfeit money[5]. They teach banks that the best defense against counterfeiting is becoming more familiar with genuine money. The logic being, if they know the real money so well, it's easier to spot the counterfeit when it arrives. They say to look for differences not similarities. This makes a lot of sense when it comes to love. The more we know real love, the better equipped we are to recognize and enjoy it, while avoiding the countless variations of counterfeit love.

Summary

Points to ponder –

Every choice we make is to gain love - directly or indirectly.

The world is full of counterfeit love which hurts people.

True love is more powerful than both faith and hope.

What would a winner do?

Be aware of, recognize, study, and learn true love.

Chapter 3
Winning at Life

I wish everyone could become rich and famous so they would find out that's not the answer either - Jim Carrey, Comedian, Actor

Motives and Expectations

Your opinion of love will determine your level of motivation for love. We are only motivated for something we *think* we really need or want. As important as oxygen is to you and me, we are not motivated for any at this moment because we have plenty. However, if we were to suddenly lose oxygen, we would be highly motivated for some - quickly. Since love is our ultimate motive anyway, I am simply suggesting that we make it our first priority, our main motive, or our surface motive. By placing our highest value and expectations on love, everything else follows for the proper reason. There's a saying - *the main thing is to keep the main thing the main thing*. When love becomes our main motive *it* completely changes our expectations.

- ❖ Decreased love <u>raises</u> expectations from the wishlist.
- ❖ Increased love <u>lowers</u> expectations from the wishlist.

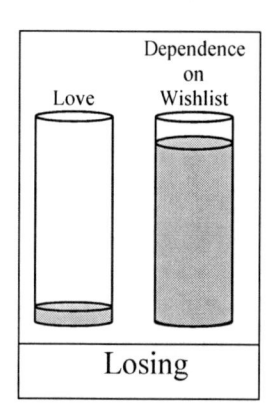

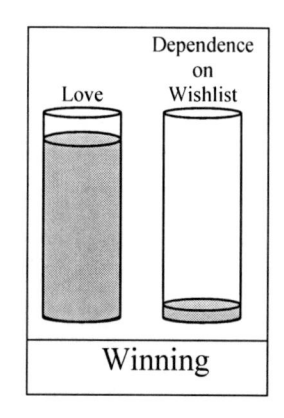

	Love	Dependence on Wishlist		Love	Dependence on Wishlist
	Losing			Winning	

Reader input: www.iwasborntowin.com/readerinput

This is not just a play on words. It is the absolute foundation to winning the most out of life. When we are low on love we attempt to get our love (or perception of love) from the wishlist. The danger of this is tremendous. If we happen to gain the wishlist without much love, we then depend upon and live from the fear of losing the wishlist. Hence, we become slaves to it. Slavery was outlawed in the U.S. a long time ago but self-slavery is very alive today, more than ever.

I personally know many slaves to the wishlist. I'll bet you do also. Watch them when they start losing any of it. They become angry, depressed, fearful, and hurtful. To them, the wishlist is their main source of love. Instead of thinking we will find love on the other side of the wishlist, we can start with the love we have right now, increase it, and then <u>enjoy</u> the wishlist. One is a victim to the wishlist while the other is a victor over it. Put your expectations on love first, then your winning will increase.

Risk and Expectations

When we expect value from something, we are taking a risk. We expect the car to start in the morning. We expect to have our job tomorrow. We expect to make it to work without being involved in an accident. If those expectations are not met we experience pain and stress, to one degree or the other. One definition of stress is the difference between actual results and expected results. Where there is risk you will find stress.

It would be painful if I were to accidentally bump into my daughter and she responded by calling me bad names. If, on the other hand, I bumped into a stranger who treated me that way, it would be far less painful. Why? While the results are the same, different expectations cause different pain. I expect love from my daughter and do in fact receive love from her. I do not expect much love from the stranger.

My daughter is actually part of my wishlist, "L" – lasting relationships. There is risk involved when I expect to receive love from her, but no risk when I *give* her love. Am I saying we shouldn't expect to receive love from other people? No, I'm not. I am saying, however, we have the ability to give and experience love directly

Chapter 3: Winning at Life

from love itself. Co-dependency consists of this very challenge. When we are constantly co-dependent on someone else to make us happy, joyful, or feel loved we end up hurt. No one else can make us happy.

I realize we must take risks in life and we will always want love from others. We will, to a degree, have expectations in things and people. But the more we do, the more we lose. As we discussed in the introduction, we must lose in order to enjoy winning. Most of us have the losing part figured out completely. False expectations must be the exception and not the rule in order to win more.

When you decide that your main value comes from love (change expectations from wishlist to love) you get to wake up tomorrow with more peace and joy. You do not have to depend on where you work, what kind of home you live in, how educated you are, or any other materialistic value. The main thing you get to depend on is gaining your value from love and increasing it (we cover the increasing details in part three). Everything else will follow. It can start happening now.

In the following chart, we clearly see real-life examples of how the same action produces different results. It all depends on why we do it and what we expect from it.

Action	Expecting and depending on the wishlist — **Losing**	Expecting and depending on love — **Winning**
Buy a new car	Get from point A to B. Must be able to make me feel important, worthy, valuable, and loved. Willing to pay higher price even if I can't afford it.	Get from point A to B. Luxuries are optional *if* they comfortably fit in my budget. Will only pay fair price.
Relationships	Other person must make me feel good, warm, fuzzy, needed, joyful, and loved. If and when they make mistakes I will feel unloved and depressed.	An opportunity to give love. *Then* love is experienced and obtained.

Reader input: www.iwasborntowin.com/readerinput

Action	**Expecting and depending on the wishlist** Love Wishlist **Losing**	**Expecting and depending on love** Love Wishlist **Winning**
Help someone else	To be recognized. Manipulation. Ulterior motives. Other person must do something for me.	Opportunity to give love, which returns love.
Eat	Survival. Energy. Feels good. Socialize. Depressed. Coping with pain. Bored. Escaping.	Survival. Energy. Enjoyment.
Work	Must make as much as possible, work overtime. Settle for what's available. Always afraid of losing job. Slave to employer. Fudge on integrity when needed.	A Means for fulfilling our purpose in life and providing a living.
Results	**This motive causes more pain and less love**	**This motive adds more love**

I realize the above samples do not apply in all situations. But I am also confident that you can relate to these motives and expectations.

You can apply this change right now. Most of us have areas of our life we depend on for the wrong reasons. They end up controlling us and before we know it we've spent most of our life being slaves to the wishlist. How many more stories must we hear of regrets and confessions from people lying on their death bed? Most say they wished they had spent more time with the kids, did more for family and friends, helped more people, and loved more. We hear this all the time. Surprisingly, we know the end of the story yet we constantly put more value in the wrong things. Seeking the wishlist is fine and part of life. You can have some of the wishlist with little love, but you can't have all of the wishlist without lots of love. Just make this one change if you haven't done so already. Seek the wishlist with love instead of seeking love with the wishlist. One road makes us a victim, the other a victor.

| Losing | Winning |

Love will give you *improved* Wellness
Love will give you *better* Information
Love will give you *more* Serenity
Love will give you *more* Hope
Love will give you *longer* Lasting relationships
Love will give you *enough* Income
Love will give you *enough* Security
Love will give you *better* Targets in life.

Winning Defined

The Webster dictionary defines winning several different ways - *to get possession of by effort or fortune, to obtain by work, to be the victor in, to reach by expenditure of effort.* Whether it's obtaining a tangible prize or an intangible feeling, the common theme in winning is *obtaining*. There's such an awesome experience and feeling of accomplishment, worthiness, and value that comes with winning – if the motive is proper.

Winning in life can literally be summed up as *obtaining love*. We've already recognized that love trumps all. Love is so powerful the Bible says it even drives out fear![6] The more love we obtain the more we win. Fortunately, there's an unlimited source of love for all of us and the choice to access it is ours.

It's impossible for me to know how much you feel loved at this moment. However, here's what I believe. Even if there are times that you feel unloved, you still have love in you. Since love is stronger than anything else - if we are living then we have some level of love inside of us. In the past, I've felt so low it would have been difficult for me to believe this, but truth is truth. If love was only around when we felt good, could it possibly have the value it has? When I was at my lowest in life, I started with love, nothing else. The little love I had gave me faith and hope for obtaining more. At that very moment, I realized I was winning a little and could use what I had to start winning more. This is what excited me so much then and still excites me today.

It doesn't matter who you are, where you are in your journey of life, what's in your bank account, or where you sleep. You have some winning inside of you right now. It doesn't matter if you're a CEO or an inmate…or both. Today, if you haven't already, you can choose to see life for what it really is - a pursuit of love. Today, you can decide that love is both the foundation and desire of life. It's at the bottom and it's at the top. You don't win more by crossing the finish line; you win more by crossing the starting line. You have the ability to win more, starting now.

The Cycle of Life

I would like to summarize what we've discussed so far with an, all too familiar, cycle of life.

1. *We exercise free will and make either right or wrong choices.*
2. *Right choices move us closer to winning.*
3. *Wrong choices take us away from winning.*
4. *Less winning means more dependence on the wishlist.*
5. *Too much dependence on the wishlist gives us unrealistic expectations.*

Chapter 3: Winning at Life

6. Unrealistic expectations result to pain.
7. As the pain increases, it becomes harder to win.
8. We avoid or deaden the pain with alcohol, tobacco, drugs, sex, money, work, sleep, food, religion, sports, gambling, shopping, spending, relationships, and many other crutches and addictions.
9. This creates more pain so we start going in circles with step 8.
10. As the pain increases, it becomes harder to win.
11. We spend more time avoiding or treating pain instead of obtaining love.
12. This takes us opposite of winning and why we were born!

Phew, what a roller coaster! Did any of that look familiar to you? I have personally been buried in that cycle before. As I've already said, I am so excited about winning and being free! That cycle could also be labeled as the rat race because they both have similar results. Unfortunately, the one who wins at the rat race is simply the number one rat. The end of that cycle leaves us at a fork in the road of life. We choose one way or the other.

1. We continue to avoid the pain and go further from winning.

- or -

2. We reverse the cycle in order to experience more winning.

Perhaps, like me, you have been down this road before and have already chosen step two. Maybe you're reading this to enjoy more of the winning life that you are currently experiencing. Or maybe you've swayed back and forth and you're ready again.

Speaking of swaying, it reminds me of the intoxicated man who swayed back and forth in the road. The police officer asked him could he not see the arrows in the middle of the road. *"Not only can I not see the arrows, I can't see the Indians either,"* replied the drunk man.

How Do We Win More

Since we are identifying winning with love, it's not likely you will ever get tired of winning. Rarely do we hear someone say they're just sick and tired of obtaining love. You don't have to wait around for your ship to come in. It's available as soon as you are. Winners don't spend their whole life trying to win. They start winning now in order to enjoy the rest of their life. Winning at life is not a speed race; you get to go at your own pace. Anyone can choose to participate. No other person can take this opportunity away from you. The world has miles and miles of the winner's highway waiting for you to travel. No one will drag you, you must jump on. Have you noticed when we go out in life looking for a friend they're hard to find? But when we go out in life to *be* a friend they're everywhere!

We must go out in life to be winners. Do you remember what the late John F. Kennedy, thirty-fifth President of the U.S., said? *"Ask not what your country can do for you but what you can do for your country."* Try this one: *"ask not how life is treating you but how you are treating life."* The answer to that question has a ton of wisdom specific to you. Here are the steps to be more of the winner you were born to be; spoken by you in the first person present tense.

- ❖ I Grow from the inside

- ❖ I Give on the outside

- ❖ I Gain from my pain

- ❖ I Gauge my growing, giving, and gaining

When executed, these steps will enable you to see areas of your life that would otherwise be invisible.

Part II: I Grow From the Inside

Chapter 4
Inner Growth

While we may not be able to control all that happens to us, we can control what happens inside us. – Ben Franklin, American Scientist

The Dead Sea is so named because it's, uhm, dead! There's no life in this sea. It brings in water and keeps it. It never gives any back, only takes. Thriving rivers give out as much as they take in. Therefore, they are fresh, alive, and healthy. The act of giving will always outlive the act of taking. But, you must first have something to give.

Who Needs Me

You may ask, *"what if my life is full of troubles?"* If it wasn't, you would not be alive. The very fact we all have trouble is what makes it possible for you and me to win more. The world actually wants you to win more. Do you get this? Others desire to win, to be loved, just like you and me. The goal is to get together and fill each other's desires. The world needs you whether you know it or not. God created it this way. Simply put, when you deliver a hug to another person it comes with a value they can never get by hugging themselves. You have enough inside of you right now to get started. Even the smallest act takes you one step closer.

Imagine if you will, you and I are the only two people left on earth. We both want to feel loved by another human. The only way to feel loved is by giving it, right? If you and I did not get together and give (be it large or small), wouldn't it be literally impossible to experience any love from each other? This means we need each other. That is what makes the world go around. People need you! Remember those expectations we discussed earlier? There are people who need so badly for you to love them. The world is full of empty hearts. You and I get to win by filling those hearts.

Are You Running on E – Ego

To get on the winning path and fill those hearts, we must get our energy from the proper, inner, fuel tank. We have two different tanks that are constantly being filled. One side is *losing*, the other is *winning*. Perhaps you're familiar with a dual-tank truck. When one tank runs out you simply switch to the other (the reserve). In life, you and I run from one inner source or the other. If we are full of anger, hatred, selfishness, and fear; guess which fuel source dominates us? Fortunately, there are many fuel stations in life to help us grow. It's important that we feed ourselves with the good, the clean, the pure, and the positive.

Ego	God
Flesh	Spirit
Insecurity	Security
Fear	Love
Losing	**Winning**

One makes us empty. The other makes us full. The biggest challenge we face is consistently fueling up with the right stuff.

Whether you realize it or not, you're more of a winner right this moment than you were prior to reading this book. You're *growing from the inside.* You're choosing to feed you. It's quite possible at this very moment you feel more energized, more hopeful, and/or more confident. You're fueling up for the winners' highway.

> "Like all living organisms, we're constantly growing or dying. I prefer to grow"

Chapter 4: Inner Growth

Just as a plant or tree must be fertilized, watered, nurtured, and maintained in order to grow, so must we. I've yet to see a dead tree give any fruit. Like all living organisms, we are constantly growing or dying. I prefer to grow and I bet you do as well.

Self-maintenance or Selfish

If you've ever flown on a plane, then you've probably heard a flight attendant say, *"In the event there's a loss of cabin pressure, oxygen masks will drop from the ceiling. If you're traveling with a small child, secure your own mask first then assist your child."* Sometimes I repeat that announcement when I'm speaking to an audience. Then I ask people who they would tend to first, themselves or their child. Most will inevitably say they would place the mask over the child's face first. This is exactly opposite of what we are supposed to do. It's completely understandable because we want to protect our children. Unfortunately, this is not the best way to protect them. We're no good to our child, or anyone else, if we don't have oxygen ourself. This is why self-maintenance is so important.

> "When we neglect self-maintenance, we actually become more selfish."

Many people are confused with selfish vs. self-maintenance. We've been so warned of selfishness that we often mistake it for self-maintenance. The fact is, where you don't have one, you have the other. The more self-maintained you are the less selfish you have to be. Your inner fuel tank will be consumed with one or the other. When we neglect self-maintenance, we actually become more selfish. If we allow guilt to stop us from being self-maintained, ironically we will experience guilt because of being selfish.

The Gas Chamber

During basic training in the Army, I was exposed to the infamous gas chamber. Trainees are taught about chemical warfare and the value of the equipment used to protect them from the burning, suffocating, life-ending gas that could be faced in wartime. The Army really wants you to appreciate the equipment, especially the gas mask. One of their ways of driving home this point is to give you first-hand exposure to the gas (CS gas). Arguably, this particular gas is said to be non-lethal. But trust me, long enough exposure will have you wanting to die! This is how I remember the event as an 18-year-old in 1985.

The rules were simple. When the drill sergeant stood in front of me, I needed to take off my helmet, place it between my knees, and hold it with my legs. Then I was to remove my mask, call out my company name, rifle number, and social security number. After this, I was supposed to put my mask back on in order to continue breathing. Then put my helmet back on top of my mask, walk out of the tent, and begin life again! As a last minute reminder, just before entering the tent, they pointed out once again to remember that our helmet is only pushed down on our mask. It wasn't fastened because the straps were not long enough to go around the mask. A helmet is a crucial piece of equipment in combat. If it were to fall off it may be difficult to retrieve in environments where visibility is limited.

We filed into a large tent, a dozen at a time, two separate lines, one behind the other. The tent was sealed very well. There was so much gas that it looked like fog. The gas was very thick, very hot, and literally started burning any exposed skin immediately. By the time the drill sergeant reached me, my skin was already burning. We were not wearing any of the body-protection equipment, only our masks. This was another reminder that they really wanted us to fear and respect the gas. They were very successful with me!

As he asked for my social security number, I noticed some of the other poor souls in the tent were running out. Like a scared bunny, and now a very burning young man, I proceeded to remove my mask so I could answer the drill sergeant. The first thing I saw was the blurred face of the drill sergeant through the foggy gas. Then I heard a thump, and the second thing I saw was my helmet rolling across the ground *because I forgot to secure it between my knees!* I immediately hit the ground. At this moment, the drill sergeant wasn't concerned about my social security number because he was too busy chewing on the remaining part of me that had survived the gas. "Where's your helmet boy? You will die in combat without your helmet. Put your helmet between your legs now!"

Chapter 4: Inner Growth

Meanwhile, I was burning, crawling, looking, and listening (in that order!). The biggest challenge was trying to focus on finding my helmet while simultaneously removing the drill sergeant's teeth from my rear end. He really wanted me to learn the proper way. I think they call that tough love. I looked, fumbled, choked, and gasped for air. I experienced a burn like I had never felt before. The words of the drill sergeant were still spraying full blast and it was one of the most agonizing times of my life.

By the time I found my helmet, I was empty, drained, and in a tremendous amount of pain. To this day, that drill sergeant still has no idea of my social security number because I never made it back off the ground. Once I located my helmet, the next mission was finding an exit. After unsuccessfully finding the exit flaps of the tent, I found an opening under the sides and crawled out. The gas literally turned me inside out. I had mucus coming from places that I didn't even know were places!

Let me assure you of a certain truth. During my gas chamber experience, I had no concerns of being a *giver*. It was all about my own selfish desires at that moment. I was dying (my perception) and my immediate concern was to live. Life is full of people who are burning, dying, and full of pain. When we are dying inside and losing, we look outside of us and become takers. Our winning (giver) fuel tank becomes low while our losing (taker) fuel tank starts providing our fuel. By maintaining yourself on the inside, you are filling your winner's fuel tank, you are growing, and *then* you're more apt to take less and give more to others.

Don't Hit the Cone

Car racing schools offer vehicle spin recovery courses. They put you and an instructor in a vehicle with four bald tires. You go out to a fairly large, wet parking lot that has an orange traffic cone in the middle. The instructor tells you to drive directly towards the cone and make a sharp turn so the vehicle will start spinning. Then you're told to recover from the spin and don't hit the cone. It seems pretty easy considering all the space in the large parking lot and only one small cone. So the driver steers toward the orange cone, turns the wheels as far as it will go, hits the brakes, and the vehicle starts spinning. The

Reader input: www.iwasborntowin.com/readerinput

orange cone can actually be seen through the windshield flying from side to side and as the driver recovers, he or she hits the cone. The drivers try again knowing for certain they will succeed the next time, considering the large parking lot and such a small cone, but they hit it again!

The instructor asks the frustrated driver to try it again. The Skip Barber Racing School says the average driver hits the cone six times. Finally, the instructor will tell the driver they're hitting the cone because they're looking at the cone. Uhhmm, excuse me? Then the instructor will continue by saying that in order to avoid hitting the cone the driver must look elsewhere. The driver is told to *look where they want the vehicle to go*. Inevitably, the driver will still hit the cone the next few runs because it's actually hard to not look at the cone. As the driver trains their eyes to look where they *want to go* rather than where they don't want to go, they end up where they want to be.[7]

"In the long run, men hit only what they aim at. Therefore they had better aim at something high." -Henry David Thoreau

It's easy to keep our eyes on the orange cones of life - the things we do not want to hit. Things like failures, regrets, fears, worries, hurts, habits, anger, frustrations, and guilt. We get it from all angles - the news, movies, sitcoms, documentaries. Negativity is all around. It takes effort, discipline, commitment, and hard work to keep your eyes where you want to go.

They're the Same Way Here

There was a man who moved into this old fashioned town. The first day he was there he met his new mail carrier. "How do the people treat you in this little old town?" the man asked. "How did they treat you in the town you just moved from?" replied the mail carrier. "They were some of the meanest, most hateful, and nastiest people I've ever been around" replied the newcomer. "They're about the same way here" said the mail carrier.

A few days later the mail carrier met another newcomer. She was also curious. "How do the people treat you around this town?" she asked. "How did they treat you where you came from?" replied the mail carrier. "They were some of the sweetest, most helpful, and caring

Chapter 4: Inner Growth

people I have ever met" replied the woman. "They're just like that here as well, you will love them" said the mail carrier.

We find what we are looking for in life. You and I must see a winner before we will be a winner. This does not take a fake person. It takes a faithful person. We must have faith in ourselves. Abraham Lincoln said a person is about as happy as they make up their minds to be.

Summary

Points to ponder-

What fuel source runs your actions the most? Losing or winning?

Do you keep your eyes (vision) pointed where you want to go in life?

Are you selfish or self-maintained?

What would a winner do?

Feed myself with the good, the clean, the pure, and the positive.

Start with what I have now, and then move forward.

Constantly look for ways to grow.

Chapter 5
Self-Image

The self-image is the key to human personality and human behavior. Change the self-image and you can change the personality and behavior. – Dr. Maxwell Maltz, American Plastic Surgeon

Have you ever noticed that it's pretty easy to lose, yet it takes effort to win? Ah, *effort*. Therein lies a challenge, at least an initial challenge. I say *initial* because, eventually, quite the opposite takes place. Losing ends up becoming extremely difficult while winning becomes very rewarding. If both losing and winning take effort, it seems reasonable we would want to refocus our efforts toward winning. This is exciting because, ultimately, it takes no more effort to win than it does to lose. It does, however, require *refocused effort*. Before you and I will attempt to refocus our efforts we must be willing to see a different view. Seeing a different view requires seeing a different you.

See a Winner

You were born to win and it helps each time you tell yourself "I was born to win." Will you try it right now and *believe* it? I_____was born to win. Or I_____was born to *obtain love*.

If you want to win more it's important that you start seeing yourself as a winner right now and not depend on what's going on around you at this moment. Your surroundings can and will change as soon as you change the way you see yourself. I've learned my body will only consistently go where my eyes can see. Even for a person who's physically blind, they "see" with other senses so they can move forward. Until we see ourselves as winners, we won't choose to win. We can stumble through life and settle but we are capable of so much more. God gave you an inner desire for more than just "getting by."

Seeing yourself as a winner, you not only consciously choose to move that way, you subconsciously choose as well.

There have been several studies claiming Police Officers are at a much higher risk of being struck, while parked, by passing traffic if the flashing lights of their vehicle are left on. It's called the "moth effect." Just as a moth flies towards the light, we unknowingly have a tendency to move towards the flashing lights. The strongest impressions in our minds will always win. If the impression in our mind is one of a poor self-image, it will dominate over things that happen outside of us. Even if we obtain all the wishlist in the world, without a healthy self-image, things could actually get worse. Why? Back to those expectations we discussed in chapter three.

> "Increasing net worth does not increase self-worth."

Lottery winners are perfect examples of this very awakening truth. Ironically, many multi-million dollar winners will end up poorer, more miserable, and lower on self-image than they had prior to receiving the money. There are many factors for this but self-image has a huge role. Suddenly receiving a bunch of anything, especially without having to <u>give</u> anything in return, will not guarantee a higher self-image. This means we will still live out the picture in our mind. In the south we have a saying that says, *"You can take the boy out of the country but you can't take the country out of the boy."* You can give all sorts of things to a person but they will still end up exactly where they see themselves ending up. Type in "lottery winner" on the internet and you will be surprised to read horror story after horror story. Not because winning the money is bad. Rather, it's the result of expecting greatness to come from outer change without making any kind of inner change. It's a recipe for disaster.

Instant professional athletes, movie stars, rock stars, and others are also an example of this. For many of them, just when they think they have the world in the palm of their hand, they end up in trouble. Or back in trouble. Why? Because increasing net worth does not increase self-worth. Let's say I see myself as inferior, less fortunate, full of anger, and a victim of society, but then I suddenly hit it "big." Now I am suddenly a rich, famous, or popular *inferior, less fortunate, full of anger, victim of society.*

Chapter 5: Self-Image

Derwin "Dewey" Gray was an NFL football player for the Indianapolis Colts. In August 1997, his fifth year in the NFL, at the pinnacle of his success, he said he looked in the mirror. "*I saw an empty, scared, selfish, wounded little boy. I had all the toys and trinkets that culture said I should have but I was missing something. I escaped the ghetto of my environment but I didn't escape the ghetto of my soul.*" Today, Dewey shares his experience with others and his purpose is now in ministry and personal growth.

Fortunately, self-image works on the positive side as well. With a healthy self-image, you can see yourself as a winning, joyful, kind, giving, and significant member of society. Then suppose you suddenly go through a divorce, lose a job, a business, or hit a huge storm in life. A decrease in net worth does not lower your self-worth. You simply become *a winning, joyful, kind, giving, and significant member of society* who is going through a storm in life. Do you see how exciting it is when we grow on the inside and do not depend on the outside? One of the best ways to increase our self-image is by looking all the way back to our beginning.

In the Beginning

The process and miracles of childbirth are quite fascinating. A small amount of matter, small enough that a million of it can fit on the head of a pin is transferred from your father to your mother. Then, approximately nine months of living, forming, and growing in a dark, wet, blurry, and noisy environment, *you* were born. Adding to the amazement, of the several billion people who have ever been born, God created you completely different than any other human being who has ever or will ever walk this earth. No one is just like you. Even your fingerprint, such a small piece of thin skin, is unlike any of the other billions. I haven't looked at billions of fingertips to verify this but I believe it. I have faith.

It's important for you to have a solid opinion of where you came from because it's a huge part of your self-image. Your belief of where you came from determines your belief in where you're going. Whether you believe in God or not, you still have faith. You either have faith that you evolved (theory of evolution) from other forms of life or you have faith that God created you. Neither can be proven scientifically. This is why it's called faith.

Evolution teaches that we are part of an evolving cycle. That we actually came from algae, plants, slime molds, animals, and fungi. That doesn't paint a very pretty picture (self-image) to me. Even the atheist, Bertrand Russell said, "Unless you assume a God, the question of life's purpose is meaningless." At the least, when one assumes a God they are open to the idea that a higher power created them with a plan. This gives you the freedom to see a winner, dream, hope, and fight for more.

Think about this for a moment. If a perfect God created you and me then we must be part of a *perfect plan!* If not, then we could hardly claim God is perfect. Obviously, God saw something in creating *you* as part of His plan. The image of you that constantly changes is your own, not your Creator's. It's impossible for His image of you to change because God cannot make mistakes. You came from a royal bloodline. It's okay to see yourself as the winner you were born to be!

Failure is an Event, Not a Person

Do you remember when you were a child and thought you had the world by the tail? Do you remember dreaming of what you were going to be when you grew up? Was it a doctor, athlete, model, singer, movie star, teacher, preacher, or nurse? What changes as we get older? Where do those dreams go? Why does it seem that we are more confident, bold, and daring as children than we are as adults? There are many answers like knowledge or the lack of, experience, and maturity. I believe a major change lies in how we see ourselves. As a child we see ourselves as brave, fearless, capable, and ready. Then life continues to unfold. Our self-image is continually molded through influence, environment, experiences, obstacles, and our own choices. It's a continuous process. Today your self-image is different than it was yesterday, last month, and when you were a child. Tomorrow it will be different than it is right now.

Your self-image determines your actions, and your actions determine your self-image. Our self-image determines who we marry, where we

Chapter 5: Self-Image

work, who we hang around with, how we dress, what we eat, the habits we form, and the way we treat people.

Dr. Joyce Brothers, psychologist and advice columnist, says *"You cannot consistently perform in a manner that is inconsistent with the way you see yourself."* In order to keep winning, in order to grow, give, gain, and gauge, a healthy self-image is vital. Did you give it any hesitation when I asked you to tell yourself "I was born to win?" If you're alone, I challenge you to say it out loud right now. "I was born to win." Did you feel empowered and hopeful? Or did you feel a little awkward, a little uncomfortable, or maybe even embarrassed? I hope you felt hopeful.

We've been told so many times what we cannot have in life that we often forget what we can have. Sometimes positive input can seem awkward, especially when it comes from within. We can see how good things happen to others, but it can be a different story when we look inside ourselves. Our self-image can make us feel like failures if we are not careful. Failure is an event, not a person. You treat people the way you see them, especially yourself. If you have areas in your life that you want to improve upon, then start seeing yourself differently in those areas. As hard as it may be to imagine yourself in a different light or view, it's difficult to change until you do exactly that.

Comparing

If we wanted to be happy, it would be easy; but we want to be happier than other people which is almost always difficult, since we think them happier than they are. - Charles Montesquieu, 18th century philosopher

One of the healthiest of all emotions is gratitude. When we are grateful we see ourselves in a more positive light. Gratitude tells us that we are valuable, worth it, and significant right now in our current situations. It propels us to move forward. Most of us have plenty to be grateful for if we will stop looking at others and look inside.

Comparing ourselves to others will usually bring negativity and lower self-image. In order to properly compare anything you must *look for differences*. When it comes to personal value, comparing is

Reader input: www.iwasborntowin.com/readerinput

guaranteed to keep us on a losing path. Why? We typically end the comparison with one of two false conclusions. First, we think we are not as valuable as someone else. Or secondly, we think we are better than they are. I believe the second is merely an extension of the first. Those who think they are better than others are likely creating a false sense of security to cover up their true belief of inferiority - A cancerous belief that tells them they are not as valuable as others. Such a belief can only be born out of comparing. The reality is, we are all on the same level. Until we see it this way our self-image is negatively affected.

My Name is Gossip

I have no respect for justice. I maim without killing. I break hearts and ruin lives. I am cunning and malicious and gather strength with age. The more I am quoted the more I am believed. I flourish at every level of society. My victims are helpless; they can't protect themselves against me because I have no name and no face. To track me down is impossible. The harder you try, the more elusive I become. I am nobody's friend. Once I tarnish a reputation it is never the same. I topple governments and ruin marriages. I end ministries set up by God. I ruin careers, cause sleepless nights, heartache, and indigestion. I spawn suspicion and generate grief. I make headlines, headaches, and more heartache. I make innocent people cry in their pillows. Even my name hisses. Who am I? I am called gossip. I come in many forms: church gossip, office gossip, shop gossip, party gossip, telephone gossip, and online gossip.

> "Until you love who you see in the mirror it is very difficult to love those you see outside the mirror."

Comparing and talking about others not only damages our self-image, it is one of the worst ways to spend our energy. We cannot possibly know what we are really comparing ourselves to anyway. We are not inside of the other person. We are simply judging from the surface. Therefore, we are tending to business which has nothing to do with

Chapter 5: Self-Image

winning. Focusing on things we have no control over is a guaranteed formula for losing.

Why is it so easy to get caught up in gossiping and comparing? Because they take the focus off of us. Gossiping and comparing feels good, initially, and helps us avoid or deaden pain in life – another form of drugs. Some of us do not like what we see inside ourselves. We would rather look anywhere except the mirror. Do you love who you see in the mirror? Until you love who you see in the mirror it is very difficult to love those you see outside the mirror. Sometimes we even change mirrors or views in hopes of something different. Changing the mirror will not change us, but changing the inside will change what we see in the mirror.

The CEO and the Seed

There was a successful business man who was growing old and knew it was time to choose a successor to take over the business. Instead of choosing one of his directors or his children, he decided to do something different. He called all the young executives in his company together. He said, "It is time for me to step down and choose the next CEO. I have decided to choose one of you." The young executives were shocked, but the boss continued. "I am going to give each one of you a seed today, a very special seed. I want you to plant the seed, water it, and come back here one year from today with the plant you have grown. I will then judge the plants that you bring. The one I choose will be the next CEO."

One man named Jim was there that day and he, like the others, received a seed. He went home and excitedly told his wife the story. She helped him get a pot, soil, and compost. They planted the seed. Everyday, he would water it and watch to see if it had grown. After three weeks, some of the other executives began to talk about their seeds and the plants that were beginning to grow. Jim kept checking his seed, but nothing ever grew. Three weeks, four weeks, five weeks went by, still nothing. By now, others were talking about their plants. Jim didn't have a plant and he felt like a failure. Six months went by, still nothing in Jim's pot. He figured he had killed his seed. Everyone else talked about their trees and tall plants, but he had nothing. Jim didn't say anything to his colleagues, however. He just kept watering and fertilizing the soil. He really wanted the seed to grow.

A year finally went by and it was time for everyone to bring their plants to the CEO for inspection. Jim felt sick at his stomach. It was going to be the most embarrassing moment of his life. However, Jim was secure enough within himself to do what was right. He took his empty pot to the board room. He was amazed at the variety of plants grown by the other executives. They were beautiful, in all shapes and sizes. Jim put his empty pot on the floor and many of his colleagues laughed. A few actually felt sorry for him.

When the CEO arrived, he surveyed the room and greeted his young executives. Jim just tried to hide in the back. "My, what great plants, trees, and flowers you have grown" said the CEO. "Today one of you will be appointed the next CEO!" All of a sudden, the CEO spotted Jim at the back of the room with his empty pot. He asked Jim to come to the front of the room. Jim was terrified.

When Jim got to the front, the CEO asked him what had happened to his seed. Jim told him the story. The CEO asked everyone to sit down except Jim. Then the CEO said, "One year ago today, I gave everyone in this room a seed. I told you to take the seed, plant it, water it, and bring it back to me today. All of you, except Jim, have brought me beautiful trees, plants, and flowers. Unfortunately, when you found that the seed would not grow, you substituted another seed for the one I gave you. Jim was the only one with the courage and honesty to bring me a pot with my seed in it.

The CEO looked at Jim, and then made an announcement to the young executives. "Here is your next CEO. His name is Jim!" Jim could not believe it. He wasn't even able to grow his seed. "How could he be the new CEO?" the others asked. To that the CEO replied "I gave you all boiled seeds. They were dead. It was not possible for them to grow. Therefore, Jim is the one who will be trusted as the new CEO."

The inner self knows the truth. Honesty *always* increases self-image.

Chapter 5: Self-Image

What Did You Say

One of the most powerful ways to increase your self-image is through changing your self-talk. Whether you realize it or not, you talk to yourself everyday through your thoughts. You talk to yourself more than you talk to anyone else. Daily, we say things like, *"I wonder if I'll make it on time. I sure am hungry, cold, hot, tired, bored, or excited. I wonder how I look. I could do better than him or her."* Some of us talk badly by calling ourselves things like idiots, dummy, silly, and stupid. We say things like, *"I can't believe I did that again. This is the last time. I should know better."*

According to psychologist Dr. David Stoop, we talk out loud at 150-200 words per minute (wpm). However, research shows our inner or self-talk is an astounding 1300wpm![8] The most important things you will ever say to a human are the things you say to yourself. Daily self-talk words create your future by painting the picture that paves the path you walk down today. Self-talk words literally give us the vision of which path we will travel. We can change the pictures we paint and the way we see ourselves by changing how we talk to ourselves.

For starters, you can look yourself in the mirror every day and talk to yourself with conviction. The eyes are the windows to the soul. It's difficult to look yourself in the eye every morning and night, claiming to be honest, and then constantly lie. It will take some time but Newton's third law of motion will work in your favor. It says for every action there is an equal and opposite reaction. This means, for every action there is a result, seen or not (faith/belief).

Look at self-talk like flushing your system from the world's daily negative input. By looking yourself in the eyes and feeding (speaking out loud) the good, the clean, the pure and the positive, it slowly flushes your system of the bad fuel and fills it with the good. Have you ever washed off a dirty carport or cleaned a pool filter? It's the consistent clean water that slowly washes away the dirt and eventually all you see is clean water. Tiny constant drips of water are what eventually wear holes in rocks and concrete. Taking five minutes in the morning, then again at night, to purposely wash out the negative influence helps clean our internal system.

Self-Talk

I have provided a copy of a self-talk sheet that I use almost everyday. You may download one at www.iwasborntowin.com/downloads. I can tell you without any fear of error that this absolutely does work. I used to run late all of my life - appointments, dinners, picking up my daughter, you name it. As I first started talking to myself, every time I would say "I am punctual," I would kind of laugh inside. After all, I knew I wasn't punctual - but it started weighing on me. You see, I realized that I was choosing to be late and therefore I could choose to be on time. The more I told myself I was punctual, the more I started seeing myself being on time. And guess what. I am on time more today than I've ever been in my life!

If you will buy into this idea, this simple adjustment to your day will enable you to think and say more often, "I was born to win." I got this idea from one of my favorite heroes - author and speaker, Zig Ziglar. Zig has helped positively change countless lives, and I am a huge advocate of his. I had the privilege of briefly working as an independent representative of the Ziglar company during 2005 and 2006. I've witnessed Zig's life enough to know he lives by this principle. This self-talk concept is taught all over the world by him and his company. You can download a version of Zig's self-talk card at www.ziglar.com. I read his at night and mine in the morning.

I highly suggest you read **out loud** to yourself. By doing so you not only think it, you also get to hear it. Reading it out loud also forces you to stay more focused and concentrate on what you're saying.

Chapter 5: Self-Image

Daily Self-talk

I_____was born to win. Today's a great day to be alive and I am excited about my future. I win in life by obtaining love which is done by giving love. The more love I give, the more of a winner I become. I am thankful that God created me as part of His perfect plan.

I_____am patient, kind, grateful, and satisfied. I am humble and seek knowledge. I am polite, concerned for others, and I control my temper. I remember and focus on the positive ways people treat me. I only delight in that which is good. I celebrate in knowing truth. I always protect, always trust, always hope, and always persevere.

I_____feel significant, valuable, worthy, and loved. I am honest and respectful with myself and others. I replace bad habits with good habits. I am sober and free of evil addictions. I have integrity and treat people the way I want to be treated. My self-image is healthy and improves daily. I am confident, prompt, and hard working. I see myself as a winner who makes a positive difference for the world.

I_____will constantly grow on the inside so I can give on the outside. I enjoy doing good deeds for others. I understand that pain for the proper purpose is productive. Therefore, I face my pain in order to gain from it and win more. I gauge my growing, giving, and gaining to have a clear picture of my progress. I am fearfully and wonderfully made. I constantly feed my mind, through my thoughts and daily self-talk, with the good, the clean, the pure, and the positive. I surround myself with people who are growers and givers. I reach out to the hurting.

I_____enjoy helping others win. I am a positive dreamer both day and night. Claiming, focusing, and improving on these qualities which I already possess gives me a realistic opportunity to have some of the things money will buy and all of the things money won't buy. I gain my value and self-worth from love. The more I give love, the more love will give me. By placing my expectations in love; I get to fully enjoy the wishlist of life. Love will give me improved **Wellness**. Love will give me more **Information**. Love will give me more **Serenity**. Love will give me more **Hope**. Love will give me longer **Lasting** relationships. Love will give me enough **Income**. Love will give me enough **Security**. And love will give me better **Targets** for the future. I_____was born to win by giving love.

Reader input: www.iwasborntowin.com/readerinput

You have likely heard phrases such as *"garbage in garbage out"* or *"you reap what you sow."* We claim to believe these phrases, but do we really? If you do, I encourage you to have this self-talk session with yourself daily. When you get up and right before you go to bed.

Summary

Points to ponder-

The same brush that paints your self-image paints your life.

When we gossip it hurts others, therefore *we* lose.

Instead of comparing to others, why not compare how much we're winning to how much we're capable of winning?

Since nobody else is like you - your love is unique. You have zero competition. The world is always looking for unique love.

What would a winner do?

See myself as a winner.

Only speak positively toward others - *praise people or be quiet.*

Increase my self-image through daily positive self-talk, which I read out loud.

Chapter 6
Conceive, Believe, Achieve

Whatever the mind of man can conceive and believe, it can achieve. – Napoleon Hill, American Speaker and Author

Conceive

It's fascinating that we actually achieve what we believe and conceive - ABC (achieve, believe, conceive). The encyclopedia says *thought* or *thinking* is a mental process which allows us to model the world, and so to deal with it effectively according to our goals, plans, ends, and desires.

It said *model*, which means to create, build, or construct. Wow, we can model our world with our thoughts. So, to a large degree, we can determine the outcome prior to living it, with our thoughts. That's exciting! Often times we get caught in the trap of our thoughts. Instead of thinking of things that we end up living *down to* we should think of things to live up to. Other words identified with *thought* were *cognition, sentience, consciousness, idea, and imagination.*

Imagination or *image in action* - if we see ourselves as a baseball player, then and only then, will we start thinking about it more. Once we start thinking about it we begin to model or create the outcome in our mind. That motivates us to plan, prepare, and execute towards the presumed outcome.

Have you ever noticed how people will talk mostly about what they have or what they're getting? Whether it's poverty, peace, politics, money, sex, sports, sickness, faith, family, fighting, or food - we really are what we think. The wine-o may not have many things in life but guess what he or she always has, wine. The workaholic may not have anything else in life, but they have their work. And the food addict may not have anything else, but they always have food. We may not get everything in life but the chances are great that we will get (achieve) what we constantly believe and conceive. If we constantly think about winning we are more apt to win!

Believe

You and I can change in small steps; it doesn't have to be radical or difficult. Small steps can make a dramatic difference. Just one gallon of used motor oil can ruin or destroy approximately one million gallons of fresh water. According to most extermination companies, termites do more damage than all fires, earthquakes, and hurricanes combined! They take such small bites, but they take so many of them. Through small but steady changes in our beliefs, we can slowly but surely make a dramatic difference. Please answer these questions:

- Do you believe there's something you can specifically do in the next three weeks that will make your life worse?
- Do you believe there's something you can specifically do to make your life better?
- Do you believe the choice is yours?

I've heard Zig Ziglar ask that question to thousands of people. If you answered yes, like most of them, here's what you've basically just said. "No matter how bad my past has been, and even as bad as things may be right now, there's something that I can personally choose to do right *now* that would make my future better, and the choice is mine." That, my friend, is extremely powerful. You're where you are today because of what you believe. This means, if you desire, you can change where you are today by changing what you believe.

Fortunately, you're the gatekeeper of your beliefs. Any other way would make you a victim, and victims have little hope. Victims are at the mercy of the victimizer. You've already proven that you are full of hope by answering "yes" to the above questions. Anytime we believe we can choose to make a difference for the better, we are hopeful. Believing is made up of our hopes, and it's also the proof of what we can't physically see…yet.

Achieve

To achieve, the ABC process has to start backwards, CBA.

C-Conceive B-believe A-achieve

After we have the conceiving and believing part down, then in order to achieve we will need to take action. The *achieving* seems to be the part where some of us end up on the wrong path. Notice I said the wrong path, I did not say this is where we seem to stop.

I realize some people are labeled as lazy or procrastinators, but it's usually more of their focus or direction. Some of the "laziest" people I've ever known were anything but lazy when they wanted to play or when they wanted something they were addicted to. Some folks wouldn't recognize work if it sat down beside them, yet they're still doing some type of activity. Like the one fela' replied when asked how long he had been working for his company, "ever since they threatened to fire me." A lot of people stop looking for work as soon as they find a job. Thomas Edison said *"Opportunity is missed by most people because it's dressed in overalls and looks like work."* Personally, I used to procrastinate a lot, but I always said I would quit, starting tomorrow! Some have said that tomorrow is the greatest labor-saving device ever invented.

I went off on a tangent to share some laughter with you and also to prove a point. Our daily actions must stay the course and consist of keeping parts C and B of the C-B-A (conceive, believe, achieve) cycle healthy. If not, over time, our negative actions will eventually influence our conceiving and believing. It's a constant cycle.

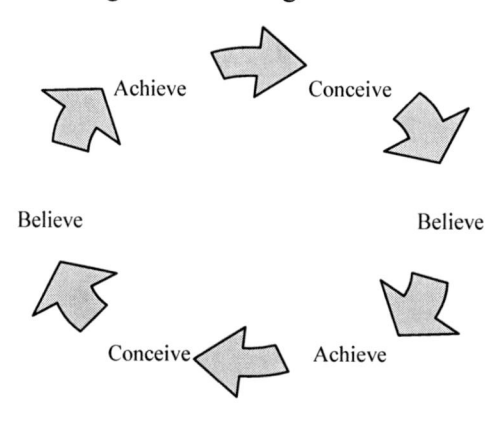

Change the Input

Since life is so busy, it's easy to overlook the need to grow on the inside. Proper maintenance will allow us to run longer, harder, and stronger. Instead of just focusing on actions, we should focus on actions that will continuously recycle, re-energize, and reaffirm our self-image. When you say "I was born to win," you complete an action that fuels other actions. You're inserting an "A" that allows more positive C-B-A. Since the C-B-A cycle runs constantly, we should be concerned with how we feed it.

When I was involved in destructive behavior, the more I did it the worse my self-image became. The worse my self-image became, the less I conceived and believed I was a winner. In return, I continued the destructive actions even more. It was a nasty downward spiral. The C-B-A cycle works to our advantage provided the input is proper. Just as the negative or destructive habits run through the loop, so does the good stuff.

Summary

Points to ponder-

Our imagination and thoughts are like a crystal ball to our future.

Our thinking has the power to take us to victimization or victory.

Do you keep your conceive, believe, achieve (C-B-A) cycle in balance?

What would a winner do?

Take negative thoughts captive and only allow good thoughts in.

Think and meditate about ways to obtain love.

Chapter 7
Forgiveness

Forgiveness is the fragrance the violet sheds on the heel that crushed it. - Mark Twain, American Humorist and Writer

Would You Forgive Him

Monday, October 2, 2006, was supposed to be another normal day at the Nickel Mines Amish School's quiet one-room school house in Pennsylvania's Dutch country. Charles Carl Roberts IV had different plans as he arrived with guns, plastic ties, and other supplies. On that day, five innocent little girls lost their lives at gunpoint, execution style, before the wicked cowardly killer shot himself.

> "Each time we forgive our past it eliminates anyone having to forgive us in the future."

Roberts wrote a note to his wife and three children, confessing he had molested two young cousins 20 years earlier and had dreams of doing it again. Also, he explained how he was mad at God for the loss of his premature daughter (Elise) in 1997. He said anytime the family would have fun he would think about Elise and what she was missing. Roberts said he would become angry and hate God more each time he thought about it.

It was an unthinkable, undeserving, and unwarranted act that took place that cold Monday morning. Of all places, a peaceful and loving community where caring and giving are so abundant. But even more unexplainable was how the Amish parents of those innocent children responded.

The blood from their daughters that lay on the schoolhouse floor was barely dry as they went to the wife of Roberts with love and support.

Their quick act to forgive the killer and also help his wife would bring about questions from even the most liberal of minds. The blank check of forgiveness, written from the hearts of the victims, quickly became the primary focus of the event. It was a rare occasion of love, faith, and courage that dominated the media outlets. How could anyone ever be so willing to forgive such a heinous act? How could they be willing to support and even raise money for the killer's family? How could they *not* become so angry and hateful? Many answers are involved, from their faith to their culture. We can be assured they had plenty of love in their hearts and they knew the value of forgiveness. The Amish people knew had they not forgiven, they themselves would experience a heart just like the hate-filled killer himself. Bitterness and anger are not discriminatory. Both will quickly fill the space of any unforgiving heart and soul. Had the killer chosen to forgive his past the Amish people could have possibly avoided the need to forgive his present. I will say that in another way. Each time we forgive our past it eliminates anyone having to forgive us in the future. The hate and anger that Roberts had came from his unwillingness to forgive.

> "As low as you think you have to stoop in order to forgive, you will always go lower if you do not forgive."

The Amish people were very hurt, they were extremely saddened and did a lot of grieving. What they were *not* willing to do was allow the killer an endless path of torture within their souls. They understood the value of forgiveness – love. They may have lost the love from their murdered children that day, but instead of losing even more from bitterness, they chose to take the winning route.

Most of us know that bitterness is bad for *us*, not the offender. Yet we insist on holding grudges against others. What is forgiveness? The word, *forgive*, in its origin means to *totally give*. I believe forgiveness is totally giving up our perceived right to hold a grudge against someone else.

Detoxification

When an addict has to stop using drugs, often times they have to go through a detoxification (detox) process. This is a process that slowly weans them off of the drugs, or the toxins. Their body is so

Chapter 7: Forgiveness

chemically dependant on the toxins that they could die if they do not go through a detox process. Being dependent on toxins (poison) will never help us grow on the inside. Bitterness and anger that occurs when we do not forgive others are poison. Bitterness can actually become a drug of choice. Like many drugs, the feeling will become so much a part of us that we come to believe we cannot live without it. If you are holding a grudge against anyone for any reason, it is possible you are addicted to the bitterness. You have possibly concluded that your life can not be as good without the bitterness. Our fears have a way of convincing us of such foolishness. There is a saying, *"fear will make you long on memory and short on forgiveness."* You may be addicted to the pleasure you get by not forgiving. Bitterness gives us power and satisfaction over the person who hurt us. But like all other drugs, it is only temporary pleasure. A person who holds a grudge is storing up anger inside, a poison. Anger, just like acid, destroys the very vessel in which it is stored. Not forgiving is like drinking poison and hoping it will kill someone else.

Harbored poisons such as anger and bitterness come out when we get squeezed. When an orange is squeezed, the only thing that comes out is orange juice. If we are full of anger, the harder we are squeezed, the more anger comes out. Unfortunately, it is usually poured on innocent people, long after the fact. What do you think this does to our self-image? Like any other drug, it slowly diminishes self-image. I am not saying it is wrong to get angry, even Jesus got angry. It is holding on to the anger that becomes dangerous. It is not easy to wean ones self off of the toxins of bitterness, but it can and must be done. The starting point is to know that forgiveness does not let the offender off the hook; it lets you off the hook. Do you have a forgiveness issue? If so, you are allowing someone else to live in your head and heart - rent free. Anger will *hinder* you the rest of your life. Forgiveness will *help* you the rest of your life. Here are three choices to assist you in forgiving: Humility – Release the grudge – Forgive ourselves

Humility

The first, and possibly hardest, step to forgiving is humility. I am convinced we have a hard time forgiving because we have been humiliated by the offender. They knock us down a "notch or two" in life. By forgiving them we may perceive we have to "give in" or "go lower." Remember the word *forgive* actually means to *totally give*. It takes lots of humility. And often times it appears to be more than we think we have, especially after we have already been humiliated. However, as low as you think you have to stoop in order to forgive, you will always go lower if you do not forgive. It is easy to think we can bury this poison. Not only will anger spew out like the orange juice illustration I mentioned earlier, it will also replace our pictures and thoughts of the future with old buried ones brought back to the surface. Anger is like a ball and chain that never goes away. It's like covering up rust with paint. If you do not cut the rust out, it eventually makes its way back to the surface.

Release the Grudge

Secondly, release the grudge. It helps us to forgive by realizing we were offended by someone who, themselves, held a grudge. We become just like our offender when we hold a grudge.

There is a great chance when people offend us; we are recipients of anger that we don't even deserve. By not forgiving, we are jumping in line with them, the *"grudge holders"* line to victimize other innocent bystanders down the road. What a vicious cycle.

I realize some of the pain is very deep and hurtful. I am not suggesting this is always easy but it is a necessary process to relieving the pressure of the pain. You can stop the destructive process. You deserve better. You deserve the peace that comes from a clear conscience. Often times, we stay angry with someone so we do not have to take responsibility for our own choices. We do not want to blame ourselves, so we keep thinking of all the faults of the other person. Growing from the inside will help you overcome such challenges and enable you to release those grudges.

Forgive Ourselves

Thirdly, we must forgive ourselves. This is very difficult and often overlooked. Our ego is wonderful at hiding this. As long as we find defects within ourselves, we will continue to act defectively. Elbert

Chapter 7: FORGIVENESS

Hubbard said *"The greatest mistake a man can make is to be afraid of making one."*

I am honored to say I've been blessed with a very forgiving spirit. But I had an issue with a man, not long ago, that bothered me for about a week. I had immediately forgiven him to his face but still felt bitterness the following week. It was an issue that should have never bothered me that long. I wrestled and prayed, trying to determine why it bothered me. I would be at the gym exercising and trying to meditate but it would dominate my thoughts. It finally struck me that I had not forgiven *me*. Why? This was not the first time I had been offended by and forgiven this individual. I felt like I let myself down by allowing him to offend me again. You have likely heard the old saying, "*Get me once shame on you. Get me twice shame on me.*" Amazingly, for the whole week, I concentrated on *his* weaknesses. What a waste of mental energy, concentrating on something I had zero control over. It almost made me hate him, yet I had truly forgiven him.

My bitterness against myself continued to magnify the shortcomings of the other person. It was as if my ego deceived me into a continuous blame game. Until I finally realized this and forgave myself, I stayed upset with both of us. Bitterness is sneaky and nasty. We should want no part of it. Bitter people hurt people, loving people love people. I was literally holding a grudge, not only against my offender but also against myself.

Quack, Quack

Johnny and Sally were visiting their grandparents one summer. Johnny had gotten a new slingshot and was out practicing in the woods, but he could never hit the target. It was finally time for dinner and as he was walking back, he saw his Grandma's pet duck. For kicks, he pulled back and let his slingshot rip. As luck would have it, he hit the duck square in the head and killed it. He could not believe it. He was sad, but most of all, he was scared. In a panic, he hid the dead duck in the bushes. Just when he thought things could not get worse, he noticed his sister Sally was watching and saw the whole incident.

After lunch the next day, Johnny's Grandma asked Sally to help with the dishes. "Grandma…Johnny told me he wanted to help in the kitchen today," said Sally. Then Sally whispered in Johnny's ear, "Quack, quack!" So Johnny did the dishes. Later that day, Grandpa asked if the children wanted to go fishing. Grandma said she needed Sally to stay and help with dinner. "Johnny told me he wanted to stay and help" said Sally, with a grin on her face. "Quack, quack," she whispered. So Sally went fishing and Johnny stayed to help his Grandma.

After several days of being manipulated by Sally, Johnny couldn't stand it any longer. He went to his Grandma and confessed that he had killed her duck. Grandma knelt down, gave him a big hug, and said, "I know you killed my duck. I was standing at the window and I saw the whole thing. But because I love you, I forgave you. I was just wondering how long you would stay a prisoner to Sally and her 'quack, quacks.'"

When we are unforgiving towards ourselves, we end up becoming a prisoner like Johnny was to Sally. Just as Grandma loved and forgave Johnny, we must do the same with ourselves. Until we are able to love and forgive ourselves unconditionally, we risk exposure to the poisons that come from bitterness. When we forgive others *and* ourselves, we open up a new door to freedom. We are saying it is ok to make mistakes in life. We are not approving the mistakes, we are accepting them. We are saying obstacles and mistakes will happen and I will learn from them. It's the difference in living life out of love rather than fear. Winners make mistakes all the time. The difference between a big shot and a little shot is the big shot is just a little shot who kept on shooting! Forgiveness allows us to leave the sidelines and play in the game of life. It allows us to say, "I was born to win," and live it.

Summary

Points to ponder-

Are you harboring any bitterness towards anyone? Why?

When we are victimized by a grudge holder, it's usually because of where we are - not *who* we are.

Grudge holders must, at some point, let go. Hopefully it's voluntary or else, innocent people are hurt.

What would a winner do?

Forgive so I can release the poison from within.

Forgive myself and use the incident to grow.

Accept the mistake so I can learn from it.

Part III: I Give on the Outside

Chapter 8
The Value of Giving

You can give without loving but you cannot love without giving –
Amy Carmichael, Irish Missionary

It's interesting and a little more than a coincidence that the neurological levels of both dopamine and serotonin (the "feel-good" chemicals) in our brain increase when we are giving. These chemicals even increase when we witness someone else giving.

I can't think of any possible way of winning in life without *giving*. I realize this should be a no-brainer. The only thing most of us are quick to give and slow to take is - advice. I'm not talking about giving material things. I mean giving ourselves, yes, love. Everything in this book is rooted around this principle. It's impossible to truly give too much. If you believe in the proven principle mentioned earlier that says *you reap what you sow,* then it's rather easy to understand that winning has a lot to do with giving. Unfortunately, when the giving gets tough many of us start taking. Therefore, you will want to make every effort to avoid *cirrhosis of the giver;* it's a losing disease.

Doing Good and Feeling Better

Half of this chapter is dedicated to an article which I think you will appreciate. It's from ABC's 20/20 which was posted Nov 29, 2006[9] by John Stossel and Sylvia Johnson.

Doing Good, and Feeling Better. *How good would it feel if someone just gave you $1,000? A few weeks ago, Oprah Winfrey thrilled audience members with these words: "You will each go home with $1,000." Then she said there was a catch: "You have to spend the money on someone other than your family."*

Winfrey said she wanted them to experience how good it feels to give. They still applauded, but the smiles looked a little forced. Yet maybe she did her audience a favor, because even though the audience had to give the money away, it could get back even more than they gave.

Stephen Post explains why in his soon-to-be released book, "Why Good Things Happen to Good People." He reveals that new science shows giving — money or time — not only feels just as good as getting, but can actually improve your health. "Giving is as good for the giver as it is for the receiver. Science says it's so. We'll be happier, healthier, and even — odds are — live a little longer if we are generous," Post said. "Public health isn't just about bugs and staying away from lead. It's about doing unto others, and at the right dose, science says it's very good for you," he said.

Arthur Brooks, author of the new book, "Who Really Cares: The Surprising Truth about Compassionate Conservatism," also knows a lot about the current research on charity. Brooks said, "There's evidence that it helps people with their asthma, in cardiovascular disease, weight loss, and insomnia. When people have a lot of happiness, they do a lot better in their health as well"- helping others, healing themselves.

That was true for former heart patients at Duke University Medical Center. They were asked to visit current heart patients — no particular agenda, just to listen and lend support. By doing that, the volunteers had better health after their heart attacks.

A similar study at the University of Miami by Dr. Gail Ironson followed HIV patients who volunteered, like Katherine Marshall Scott, who talks to teenagers about avoiding infection, and Stephen Baker, who counsels fellow HIV survivors. These and other HIV patients who helped others had lower stress levels and higher immune resistance. Scott's disease-fighting cells went up from 200 to 800. Baker says he could feel how volunteering improved his health. "To get involved with someone else's problems makes your problems look a lot less," he said.

At least five studies show that seniors who gave tended to live longer, Post said. After senior Fred Dekuyper started volunteering at a school, a small miracle happened. "I used to walk with a cane all the time, and now I don't need the cane anymore," he said.

Chapter 8: The Value of Giving

Service Learning

Many high schools require their students to volunteer. It's called service learning. And oddly, even though the charity is forced, it still brings happy results. Teachers say students who volunteer raise their grades and get higher SAT scores. Abington High School student Jeff Rohrback said, "After service learning started, I got so involved into it, I started paying attention more, picked up my grades." So "20/20" decided to see whether we could find a similar effect.

We put an ad on Craigslist® recruiting people who were not currently volunteers. We introduced them to Post and asked them to try it for one week. But first, Post had them fill out a questionnaire that asked how they felt about life, like how often during the week they felt calm and peaceful.

Children for Children, whose mission is to get children involved in giving, agreed to help us, as did the Salvation Army, which has many different programs, from soup kitchens to after-school activities for kids.

Then off they went — bringing donated books to children at an elementary school, then reading to the kids and making scarves with the kids. One spent time in a truck handing out food to the poor. All four worked at a Harlem soup kitchen. One week later we had them answer that questionnaire again.

This time their answers about how often they felt "calm and peaceful" changed from some of the time to most of the time. Post said, "In fact, just seven days of activity was a kind of a transformation." One of our volunteers, Diana Sanchez was surprised at how strongly the experiences affected her. "They were so grateful for me doing that, but it was just peas and carrots," she said. When asked whether it had made her feel good, she said, "It did/it did."

Sanchez also spent time with kids at a Salvation Army after-school program. "Just knowing that after work I was heading over to work with the children, just seeing them smiling — that just made me feel so great," she said. Researchers call that "the helper's high."

The Helpers' High

"The helper's high has been measured physically," Post said. *"We know there's an actual physiological state. It's quite euphoric."* The helper's high shows up in MRI brain scans. People who give money show brain activity that's associated with feel-good chemicals like dopamine — the same brain activity that happens when you receive money. National Institutes of Health neuroscientist Jordan Grafman showed us the brain scans. *"Those brain structures that are activated when you get a reward are the same ones that are activated when you give. In fact, they're activated more,"* he told us.

We asked our volunteers after their week of service who had gotten more out of the experience: the people they helped, or they themselves. Volunteer Daniel Smith didn't hesitate with his answer. *"No brainer, me, definitely,"* Lelani Clark also felt renewed from her single week of volunteering. *"I just felt energized,"* she said. *"We were so caught up in this energy of helping that it was like a buzz — like a spiritual buzz."* Winfrey's audience members reported that, too. After a week of giving money away, many said they were changed.

Maybe we should call it selfish to help others, because it seems to help the givers more. *"If you want to define selfishness so widely as to include the warm glow that people feel in the aftermath of selflessly giving to others, guess what, we need more of it, not less of it,"* Post said. So try it. Get out and give your money or your time. You'll help someone else... and you'll feel good, too.

Outside the Hospital Window

Sometimes we may not feel adequate but we can usually find a way to benefit others regardless of our own circumstances.

Two men, both seriously ill, occupied the same hospital room. One man was allowed to sit up in his bed for an hour each afternoon to help drain the fluid from his lungs. His bed was next to the room's only window. The other man had to spend all his time flat on his back. The two men talked for hours on end. They spoke of their wives and families, their homes, their jobs, their involvement in the military service and where they had been on vacation. Every afternoon when

Chapter 8: The Value of Giving

the man in the bed by the window could sit up, he would pass the time by describing to his roommate all the things he could see outside the window. The man in the other bed began to live for those one-hour periods where his life would be broadened and enlivened by all the activity and color of the world outside.

The window overlooked a park with a lovely lake. Ducks and swans played on the water while children sailed their model boats. Young lovers walked arm in arm surrounded by flowers of every color of the rainbow. Grand old trees graced the landscape, and a fine view of the city skyline could be seen in the distance. As the man by the window described all this in beautiful detail, the man on the other side of the room would close his eyes and vividly imagine the picture perfect scene. One warm afternoon the man by the window described a parade passing by. Although the other man couldn't hear the band he could see it in his mind's eye as the gentleman by the window portrayed it with descriptive words.

Days and weeks passed. One morning, the day-nurse arrived to bring water for their baths only to find the lifeless body of the man by the window, who had died peacefully in his sleep. She was saddened and called the hospital attendants to take the body away. As soon as it seemed appropriate, the other man asked if he could be moved next to the window. The nurse was happy to make the switch, and after making sure he was comfortable, she left him alone. Slowly and painfully, he propped himself up on one elbow to take his first look at the world outside. Finally, he would have the joy of seeing it for himself. He strained and slowly turned to look out the window beside the bed. To his surprise, it faced a blank wall. The man asked the nurse what could have possibly motivated his deceased roommate to describe such wonderful things outside this window. The nurse responded that the man was blind and could not even see the wall. She said, "Perhaps he just wanted to encourage you."

Obviously, the blind man did not think about the "have-nots," but rather, the "haves." We can all find reasons why we can't give. But if we try, we can also find ways to give with what we have, right now.

Part III: I Give on the Outside

Prevent Defense

Giving is so simple that we often miss the opportunity even when it's staring directly at us. Is it possible we miss these opportunities because of our perception of winning? Think about it, if we're convinced that the wishlist makes us a winner then we must think it makes other people a winner also. Not only will we chase the wishlist instead of love, we will also *give* the wishlist in place of love. It only makes sense that we attempt to give what we think makes the other person happy.

A father buys his son another toy (wishlist) when all along the boy just wanted his dad's time. The boss offered the employee a raise to keep her when all along it was appreciation that was missing. The girl has sex on the first date when the boy was really looking for someone with discipline and self-respect. The husband buys his wife a dozen delivered roses when a single rose from his hand to hers would mean so much more. It's almost scary when we stop and realize how difficult we make it. Love is all around, an endless supply for the giving and the taking. But we miss it because we are looking for the big stuff. When we look for ways to give the big stuff instead of giving love it's easier to become passive.

How many times have you heard a man say he doesn't have enough money to get a date? Or a woman says she isn't pretty enough? How often does a couple say they can't afford a baby? If everyone waited until it was affordable and convenient to have a child, most of us would not be here. Look at all the opportunity that's missed because we think we need to give the wishlist instead of love. We miss the tiny things because we're sitting back and waiting for the big opportunities. The NFL is a perfect example of this.

A football game consists of four quarters. At the ends of the second quarter (half time) and fourth quarter (end of game), the teams are given a two-minute warning. The clock is stopped and each team huddles together to plan their final strategy. The defensive teams are notorious for setting up in a formation known as the *prevent defense*. The strategy is to prevent the offense from making the big plays by allowing them to gain short yardage. It's a bend-but-don't-break plan. This type of thinking is based on the idea that the defense is satisfied with their results, up to this point, and as long as they don't let the other team make a big play then the small gains are okay. They focus on preventing the big plays when it's the small ones that have the most effect.

More often than not, the prevent defense strategy works against them. The other team ends up taking advantage of the "soft" approach. Little by little they gain small steps. After enough small gains by the offense, the defense usually ends up in a crunch finally realizing that the plan backfired. The famous coach and now broadcaster John Madden says, *"All a prevent defense does is prevent you from winning."* I think this applies to life. Overlooking the small things, while anticipating the big ones, is a losing strategy. On the positive side, you and I can be like the offensive team. Even if we think we're down or behind in life, we can win with small steps. Any tiny act, of giving out of love, will slowly move us closer to the "win zones" of life.

Making a Difference

What did you give today? The next page displays a list of things we tend to take for granted throughout life. These things will be remembered more than most "stuff" we chase in life. Please take a moment and circle or underline the things you *gave* today. More than we could ever realize, these are the difference makers. I encourage you to add your own.

"Anyone can tear things and people down, but those who build things and people up go up themselves." -Zig Ziglar

You will feel more purposeful and full of joy after you stop to think about how you make a positive difference in the world. If you can't highlight many from the list right now, try to come back and look at it again tomorrow. I encourage you to add some of your own.

Part III: I Give on the Outside

Today, I made a difference by giving:____ or because I:____.

A smile	Friendly advice	Sang to someone
A touch	Protection	Read to someone
Word of encouragement	A shoulder to cry on	Visited a retirement home
An ear to listen	Comfort	Wrote a note
A handshake	Security	Hope
A touch	An opened door	Inspiration
A compliment	A helping hand	Gave a donation

I hope you added a few of your own. Isn't it wonderful to know that most of the things listed can't be bought? That's one of the most awesome things I enjoy about the art of giving. It costs so little and returns so much. It is by far one of the best investments any of us can make.

Summary

Points to ponder-
Giving increases the "feel-good" chemicals in our brain.
The giver is the bigger winner.
Like the blind man next to the window, we should use what we have.
Give the small stuff; it's what ultimately matters anyway.
Love is wrapped up in the small stuff, all around, ready to be given.

What would a winner do?
Look for tiny ways to give every day.

Chapter 9
Paradigm Shifts

Seek first to understand, and then to be understood.
— Stephen R. Covey, American Lecturer, Author

Learning to see things the way others see them definitely helps us become more effective at giving. Each of us sees life in a completely different view. It's difficult for any two people to see the *exact* same thing because we are looking with different eyes, emotions, memories, thoughts, and perceptions. A baseball bat to one may paint a picture of a fun night at the ball park. To another it may paint a nightmare from a beating. With effort and practice, despite our differences, we're capable of seeing *similar* views.

A paradigm shift is that similar view. It means I deliberately try to see it the way you see it, a different perspective. Or, as we say in the small town where I grew up, I switch winders (windows). Figuratively speaking, I am willing to temporarily walk away from the window of life that I'm currently looking through and attempt to see life through your window.

It takes inner security (love) to even be willing to make a paradigm shift. It means you're giving up your right of view in order to attempt to see (understand) how the other person sees it. Winners are extremely good at this. It's one of the most powerful tools for communicating. There's a saying: *When you change the way you see things, the things you see will change.*

The Difference between You and Me

The following was excerpted from the book "Please Understand Me II" by David Keirsey, PhD[10].

If I do not want what you want, please try not to tell me that my want is wrong. Or if I believe other than you, at least pause before you correct my view. Or if my emotion is less than yours, or more, given the same circumstances, try not to ask me to feel more strongly or weakly. Or yet if I act, or fail to act, in the manner of your design for action, let me be. I do not, for the moment at least, ask you to understand me. That will come only when you are willing to give up changing me into a copy of you.

I may be your spouse, your parent, your offspring, your friend, or your colleague. If you will allow me any of my own wants, or emotions, or beliefs, or actions, then you open yourself, so that some day these ways of mine might not seem so wrong, and might finally appear to you as right - for me. To put up with me is the first step to understanding me. Not that you embrace my ways as right for you, but that you are no longer irritated or disappointed with me for my seeming waywardness. And in understanding me you might come to prize my differences from you, and, far from seeking to change me, preserve and even nurture those differences.

Excuse Me, May I Help You

This is a true story that I experienced one morning while I was eating. I was having breakfast at this little café down the road from my house. I was reading the newspaper as I ate and noticed out of the corner of my eye a young man who came and sat in the seat catty-corner to me. "Good morning," we both said. In just a few minutes, I noticed him staring at me. I continued to read the paper. He kept staring, I kept reading and eating.

I don't know if I have Attention Deficit Hyperactivity Disorder (ADHD) or not but I do, at times, find it difficult to concentrate. He wasn't making it any easier. I'm typically a simple person to get along with so I had no intention of making a scene. Usually, I would even start chatting with a person in this situation - but I was trying to eat, read, and concentrate.

The young man started sliding closer in an attempt to read my paper. As he continued to slide closer he was now, kind of, hovering over my food. I still think I'm simple to get along with but I would prefer

Chapter 9: Paradigm Shifts

if something were to drop in my food that it come from my own hands, face, or head. Can I get an Amen?

I was starting to feel a little uncomfortable with this man leaning into my space the way he was. After practically leaning in and almost sliding me out of my own chair I finally asked, "Excuse me, may I help you?" "Yes you may," he said with a crackling voice. "I am trying to see if my brother is in the newspaper like they said he would be." Then I noticed his eyes were becoming glossy. "He was in a helicopter in the Iraq War and got shot down two days ago. He died." I *gladly* helped the young man.

Have you noticed how your mood and thoughts about the man just changed? They likely went from gross to sympathetic, immediately. This is the awesome power of a paradigm shift. What mattered seconds ago no longer matters. Now it doesn't matter that he was practically leaning on me and my plate of food. What changed?

The man didn't change, the food didn't change, and my rights didn't change. What did change was enough information. It was the extra information that allowed you and me both to stop looking at life through our window. The window that says, "I would shove him away or move away." Instead, we move over to his window and see a different picture. A picture of pain and sorrow that said, "This poor guy is hurting and is simply looking for relief."

Wow, isn't it amazing how you immediately want to help this guy, the same guy who was a "jerk" just moments prior? He was only a jerk until we did a paradigm shift. The more we are able to see life through the windows or eyes of another, the more we are willing to give. *Change the way you see things and the things you see will change.*

Please Hear What I'm *Not* Saying

Givers look for ways to have paradigm shifts even when they don't have all the information. Fortunately, the man I met at breakfast was hurting so bad that he was willing to spill his heart with me. But more often than not, people won't give us any extra information. This is where true winners are recognized. We have to constantly be willing

Part III: I Give on the Outside

to look at life through the other person's eyes, even when they're not giving us the cues. The following will illustrate this quite well[1].

Don't be fooled by me. Don't be fooled by the face I wear. For I wear a mask, a thousand masks, masks that I'm afraid to take off because none of them are me. Pretending is an art that's second nature with me, but don't be fooled, for God's sake don't be fooled.

I give you the impression that I'm secure, that all is sunny and unruffled within as well as without. I pretend that confidence is my name and coolness is my game. That the water is calm and I'm in command and need no one. But please do not believe me.

My surface may seem smooth but my surface is my mask, ever varying and ever concealing. Beneath lies many concerns. Beneath lies confusion, fear, and aloneness. But I hide this; I don't want anybody to know it. I panic at the thought of my weakness exposed. That's why I frantically create a mask to hide behind, a nonchalant sophisticated facade that enables me to pretend. It shields me from the glance that could possibly know the truth.

But such a glance is precisely my salvation, my hope, and I know it. That is, if it's a look of acceptance and it's followed by love. Love is the one sure thing that can liberate me from myself, from the barriers I so painstakingly erect, from my own self-built prison walls. It's the only thing that will assure me when I can't assure myself that I'm really worth something.

But I don't tell you this. I don't dare; I'm afraid to. I'm afraid your glance won't be followed by acceptance; that it won't be followed by love. I'm afraid you'll think less of me, that you'll laugh, and your laugh would kill me inside. I'm afraid because deep down I need to feel valuable and you might see this and reject me.

So I play my game, my desperate pretending game, with a facade of assurance on the outside and a trembling child within. So begins the glittering but empty parade of masks and parts of my life becomes a front, a fake. I tell you everything that's really nothing, and nothing of what's everything, of what's crying within me.

So when I'm going through my routine, do not be fooled by what I'm saying. Please listen carefully and try to hear what I'm not saying, what I'd like to be able to say, what for survival I need to say, but what I can't say. I don't like hiding. I don't like playing superficial phony games. I want to stop playing them. I want to be genuine and spontaneous and be me, but you've got to help me.

You've got to hold out your hand even when that's the last thing I seem to want. You can be the one to wipe away from my eyes the blank stare of the breathing dead. You can be the one to call me into aliveness. Each time you're kind, gentle, and encouraging, each time you try to understand because you really care, my heart begins to grow wings. Very small wings, very feeble wings, but wings nonetheless.

With your power to touch me into feeling, you can breathe life into me. I want you to know this. I want you to know how important you are to me, how you can be a creator--an honest-to-God creator--of the person that is me, if you choose to. You can be the one to break down the wall behind which I tremble. You can be the one, that special one, to remove my mask. You can release me from my shadow world of panic, from my lonely prison, if you choose to.

Please choose to. Please don't pass me by. It will not be easy for you. A long parade of masks can give a conviction of worthlessness which builds strong walls. The nearer you approach to me the blinder I may strike back. That may seem irrational, but despite what the books and experts say about humans, often I am irrational. I fight against the very thing I cry out for. But I am told that love is stronger than strong walls and in this lies my hope. Please try to beat down those walls with firm hands, but with gentle hands for a child is very sensitive.

Who am I, you may wonder? I am someone you know very well. For I am every man, woman, or child you will ever meet.

Father's Day with Daddy

I want to share a story that's very special to me. It's an email exchange between my daughter and me. She was twelve at the time. As I mentioned in the front of the book, her name is Cassandra, but I call her "Boogie." Her mother and I share joint custody so she is not with me all the time. We had just spent a week together.

Part III: I Give on the Outside

Boogie,

I've enjoyed getting to see you this week. I love when I get to spend time with you. I would really enjoy having you with me at church on Father's Day.

I love you honey,

Daddy

Hey Daddy,

I had fun with you too. I am sorry that I can't be there on Father's Day. 🦉 ****** Cheer Camp invited our team over this weekend and I really want to go. I am sorry but I can spend some time with you this coming week.*

I love you,

Boogie

It's ok Boogie, I understand. You don't have to be sorry. I am sure you will have lots of fun. We can make it up next week. Please take some pictures and I will see you soon! Maybe you can stop in and see me Sunday night on the way back home if it's not too late. I love you Boogie, Muah.

Daddy

Initially, the conversation may appear as if we have a weak relationship. Why would a daughter not want to spend Father's Day with her dad? It's a valid question and very understandable; the exact thought entered my mind, initially. Fortunately, our relationship is so solid that the answer also entered my mind, immediately. This does not mean that thoughts of rejection or unworthiness did not enter my mind with vicious motives. It simply means they were quickly disregarded and taken captive by the truth. By knowing it's true that we have a great relationship, it allows me to look at this situation openly and rationally. She was 12 years old, I was 39. We had just spent most of the week together with a lot of extra quality time, much more than we normally spend together. In her mind, it's possible that Father's day was just another day. She can see me anytime she wants but this particular event was only for that specific weekend.

Why miss the event when she can have both? Does this sound familiar - cake and eat it too? Don't we look at our options in life, see which ones we want, then try to fit them all in? It's easy to see how that's okay when it's in our favor, but when it goes against our own desires the view can seem unfair. This is another advantage of paradigm shifts. The ability for me to see through her window of life kept things in the proper perspective. It turned what could have been a daddy having a pity party into a daddy and daughter who were able to be *givers*.

Summary

Points to ponder –

No two people see anything exactly the same.

When's the last time you took an interest in another view?

Showing an interest in a different view doesn't require yours to change. It simply means you're accepting of differences.

Paradigm shifts have the power to change emotions, thoughts, and actions.

What would a winner do?

Try to see things through the eyes or windows of others.

Seek first to understand then to be understood.

Chapter 10
Personality and Behavior

There are three things extremely hard; steel, diamonds, and knowing ones self - Ben Franklin, American Scientist

A most powerful paradigm shift is one done on ourself. It's also one of the most difficult to accomplish. How many times have you seen yourself in a photo or video only to be surprised? You didn't realize you were *that* fat, skinny, funny, angry, or happy. Peak performance expert Dennis Waitley, says, *"Winners have the ability to step back from the canvas of their lives like an artist gaining perspective. They make their lives a work of art – an individual masterpiece."*

The following is based on the research of William Moulton Marston, Ph.D. (1893-1947). Marston was influenced by Carl Jung and sought to find theory to explain the behavior of people. In 1928 Marston introduced four different types of human personality and behavior. The four types are DISC (Dominant, Influence, Steady, and Conscientious). In addition to his work on personality, emotional intelligence (before it was called emotional intelligence), and behavioral styles, he is also credited with developing the lie detector. Another interesting side note is that Marston was also the creator of "Wonder Woman," where he introduced the strong female superhero into comic strips.

DISC has continued to evolve. From Marston's original development of the DISC model to the research conducted by the University of Minnesota's Dr. John Geier and other researcher and assessment developers. Over five million people have taken various forms of the DISC profile throughout the world. One of the largest publishers of DISC is Inscape Publishing®.

Determining Styles

There are no wrong or right answers when determining your personality type. You are unique and this is a tool to help you learn more about *you*. The following chart has ten different rows consisting of four words in each row. Go across each row and choose which word is **most** like you, *in your most natural state*, and assign it four (4) points. Choose the word that's **least** like you and assign it one (1) point. Assign the other two words three (3) and two (2) respectively. The top row is a sample for you to view. You should have a four, three, two, and one across every row. Please remember, any of this could be different under different situations in life. It's important to choose based on *natural tendency or second nature.* Usually, the quicker you answer, the more accurate your results will be.

Personality Determination

	Sample _3_ Determined	Sample _4_ Convincing	Sample _1_ Predictable	Sample _2_ Cautious
1	___ Determined	___ Convincing	___ Predictable	___ Cautious
2	___ Bold	___ Sociable	___ Cooperative	___ Precise
3	___ Direct	___ Expressive	___ Kind	___ Analytical
4	___ Competitive	___ Inspiring	___ Consistent	___ Detailed
5	___ Outspoken	___ Animated	___ Patient	___ Logical
6	___ Strong willed	___ Persuasive	___ Easy-going	___ Orderly
7	___ Daring	___ Outgoing	___ Agreeable	___ Careful
8	___ Restless	___ Enthusiastic	___ Considerate	___ Thorough
9	___ Decisive	___ Talkative	___ Loyal	___ Controlled
10	___ Aggressive	___ Playful	___ Satisfied	___ Accurate
	\multicolumn{4}{c}{**Totals**}			
	Dominant D	Influence I	Steady S	Conscientious C

Reader input: www.iwasborntowin.com/readerinput

Once you have assigned numbers to all ten word groups, total the points for each column and write the totals in the spaces provided at the bottom. Circle the letter under the highest score; this is your primary personality style. Put a square around the second highest, this is your secondary style.

What Style are You

D = **Dominant**; demanding**,** driven**,** and direct.

When approaching these folks, gather your thoughts beforehand. Because the Dominant person doesn't have time to wait!

I = **Influence;** interactive, inspiring, and impulsive.

When approaching the Influencers, don't worry about gathering your thoughts. You will have plenty of time, while they do all the talking!

S = **Steady**; stable, sincere, and supportive.

When you approach these people, be prepared for a group hug!

C = **Conscientious**; **c**ompliant, **c**ompetent, and **c**alculated.

When you approach these people, state your name, purpose, and expected length of visit….using proper grammar please!

People are flexible and very capable of acting certain ways in certain situations. However, our *natural* tendency is to spend more time in two of these four styles - a primary and a secondary. These are not absolutes and you may see some descriptions of your primary and secondary styles that do not apply to you. In addition, you may see things in the other two styles that do apply to you. In general, the accuracy is both powerful and intriguing.

Have you ever wondered why you do certain things the way you do them? Why you choose not to do some things even when you want to? Why it seems so easy for one person to do something but not you? Or why it seems so tough for some people but for you it's a breeze? A lot of these answers are wrapped up in your God-given personality style. Being aware of this is not intended to excuse you from challenges or from continuing to improve upon natural talent. It is to enable you and empower you to be more of the winner you were born to be. You may notice that some of these qualities or challenges no longer apply to you. The reason for this is because we change based on things like experiences, desires, perceptions, beliefs, environments, and inner growth. Once you become aware of these personality traits you can and will change for the better, if you choose to do so.

Coach Tony Dungy of the Indianapolis Colts is a good example of personality change. He is one of the most controlled, calmest, and steady football coaches in the NFL. He said he was not always like that. He used to be the guy yelling, screaming, and getting kicked out of the games for fighting. Those who know him today would not recognize many of his old personality traits.

Different Personality Styles

Dominant-D : Colin Powell, Bill O'Reilly, Tiger Woods, Donald Trump, George Patton, David Letterman, Gen. Schwarzkopf, Vince Lombardi, Bobby Knight, George W. Bush, Margaret Thatcher, and Hillary Clinton

Dominant-D's are **d**emanding, **d**riven, and **d**irect. Their primary interest is <u>results</u>. They enjoy solving problems, getting things done, and achieving goals. They want to be in charge and dislike being told what to do. They set high standards for performance on themselves and others. This means they find fault as if there's a reward for it. They are less concerned with details and more interested in results. These are the people who say "hey, don't bore me with the labor pains, show me a baby!" They can unknowingly run people over because of their high ability to focus. They are often in a hurry and impatient. Their favorite work tool is the bull dozer. These are the kind of people who watch 60 Minutes in half an hour. When they purchase a new vehicle, the first thing they want to know is how fast

Chapter 10: Personality and Behavior

it will go. They see no reason for yellow and red traffic lights, only green: go-go-go.

Dominant D's are the natural born leaders in life. They thrive on challenges and competition. They are willing to take risks, go against the grain, swim upstream, and break the rules. They make decisions quickly and are impatient with people who spend too much time talking or planning. If you do not believe this, just ask a Dominant-D because they are happy to tell you exactly what is on their mind. They can be blunt and have no problem telling you when you are wrong. The only thing they experience quicker than boredom is getting angry. They are also the best at getting over both rather quickly. When you need help facing a storm head on, you can count on the bold Dominant-D.

Influence-I : Johnny Carson, Barack Obama, Elvis Presley, Jay Leno, Zig Ziglar, Oprah Winfry, Bill Clinton, Jim Carrey, Bill Cosby, Billy Graham, Joel Osteen, and Ronald Reagan

Influence-I's are interactive, inspiring, and impulsive. Their primary interest is people. They are outgoing, charming, and optimistic. These people enjoy the scenery even on a detour. They will take their last two dollars and buy a money clip. The Influence-I is a "people person" who genuinely likes people and wants to be liked. They trust people and enjoy bringing out the best in folks. They are excellent communicators and enjoy telling stories, even when exaggeration is involved. And sometimes, especially when exaggeration is involved! They enjoy meeting new people, working with others, and networking. If you ever suggest they not be a stranger, you should prepare to see them often, especially if they like you. They tend to ignore the rules since they do not think they really apply to them anyway. They are energized by working with people and will usually energize any group they work with.

Influence-I's see the big picture and "tomorrow" is the moment they like to seize. They are the ones who intend to quit procrastinating, starting tomorrow! They dislike details and can be scattered. When their checkbook does not balance, they just change banks. One of their biggest motivators in life is the last minute. They think they can talk their way out of any crunch. They can be very inspirational and motivating. These are the people who talk on elevators when they are the only ones on the elevator. They will talk for five minutes before realizing their cell phone has dropped the call. When they have nothing to do, they want to do it with you. If you need someone to warm up the group or a public relations expert, the Influence-I is your person.

Steady-S: Barbara Bush, Tony Dungy, Mother Teresa, Florence Nightingale, Princess Diana, and Tonto from the Lone Ranger

A **Steady-S** is sincere, supportive, and stable. Their primary interest is cooperation. They are very loyal and trustworthy. When they say it's going to rain, you should grab your umbrella. They're sympathetic and understanding. They are the people behind the scenes that hold it all together. They make excellent shoulders to lean on because they are good listeners. The Steady-S is a team player that respects the way things are done. They would rather gnaw their arm off instead of go through change. The only change they like is quarters, dimes, and nickels. They enjoy stability, harmony, and group hugs. They do not like being pushed or pressured. They dislike conflict and cannot understand why boxers insist on punching each other! They think appeasement is the best solution. "Can't we all just get along," they ask. They are patient and stick with projects from beginning to completion. They try to avoid risk and believe the best way to double your money is to fold it over and stick it back in your pocket. They go with the flow and help keep everyone together. When you need support and cooperation you should look to the Steady-S.

Conscientious-C : Bill Gates, Warren Buffet, Alan Greenspan, Vijay Singh, Condoleezza Rice, Jimmy Carter, Larry King, Sherlock Holmes, and Ralph Nader

Conscientious-C is **c**ompliant, **c**autious and **c**alculated. Their primary interest is quality. They are the intellects of the world who enjoy being right. They research every aspect of a situation and consider every possibility before making a decision. They would prefer all the traffic lights are on green before leaving home. They value their reputation for being accurate and logical. They would never admit to leaving cookies out for Santa! These intellects like systems and procedures that produce predictable and consistent outcomes. Their sock drawer is orderly. They know exactly how many miles to the gallon their vehicle will get. They often look for what could go wrong and support the Murphy's Law theory. These folks think someone may have actually pushed Humpty Dumpty off the wall. They read the fine print and are sticklers for detail. They have been known to actually proofread zerox copies. They have high standards for accuracy. They even recount their money from an ATM machine. Their perfectionism can create analysis paralysis. They are so analytical they would be involved in a research study to watch paint dry, preferably alone. They do not take shortcuts and are huge on quality. When you want it done right, the Conscientious-C is your best bet.

Personality Patterns

Do you feel like we have known each other a while? Did any of your family members, co-workers, or friends come to mind? Can you see the value in this information? It is awesome to know we are able to use these patterns to help predict behavior about ourselves and others.

Perhaps your boss, mate, or friend is a Dominant-D who *runs you over* or wants to dominate you. These patterns allow you to realize this is their natural tendency and that it is not personal. As I have already stated, this is not an excuse. But it does inform us and allow us to predict behavior so we can prepare. The same Dominant-D would be wanted and desired if they were going into battle. In other words, it's all about keeping a balance between our specific strengths and needs. An overextension of a particular strength can become a need. In most cases, we are simply overusing our God-given strengths to a point of neediness or being unbalanced. Ralph Waldo Emerson said *"People with great gifts are easy to find, but symmetrical and balanced ones never."*

Overusing a Strength

Balance, as with many areas of life, is crucial when dealing with our personality. My primary personality is Influence-I and my secondary is Dominant-D. Another way to say it, a high "I" backed up by a "D", or *I/D* for short. Talking is one of my strengths. Sometimes I overuse it. Ask anyone who knows me! There are times my daughter will not ask me a question because she doesn't want to know **that** much about it. Overuse can become undesirable. Even steak or ice-cream ten times per day might be too much.

When I first started in my professional career of selling I lost many sales because I would not shut up. This does not mean I didn't sell a lot because I did. I sold my dog, my stereo, my furniture, and anything else to make ends meet! But my job was supposed to be demonstrating and selling Rainbow® Vacuums in homes. I would put on, what I thought to be, a very fun, energetic, and enthusiastic presentation. It would have been more fun, for me personally, had they been more financially profitable. I would talk and talk in order to make certain that I told the prospect everything possible before they could say *no*. I talked myself out of lots of sales as a result. My newness in the sales industry, lack of confidence, and poor self-image were the problems. These weaknesses motivated me to say as much as I could because I was *afraid* (insecure) of hearing *no*. My sales manager went over the closing with me (again) until I was comfortable. Only after I became more secure with myself was I able to stop overusing my strength.

It only makes sense that our fears, pains, or other insecurities will automatically or subconsciously force us to lean on our strengths. As with many things, too much leaning in one area can create weaknesses in others. I started getting more sales once I learned to balance my talking and use it as my strength. Prior to that, I was simply a professional visitor. As long as I made no sale, both my prospect and I lost out. Once I did some *growing on the inside,* I was more capable of *giving on the outside.*

Out of Balance

A Steady-S is typically a good listener. If this strength is overused it will create and expose a need. Then it may be like pulling teeth to get the "S" to talk. Here is what happens when we are out of balance.

Dominant-D tends to be impatient and/or blunt to the point of being rude. They can be a bully, a loudmouth, and a controller. Like a tidal-wave, they run over people's feelings. They are prone to be very critical, demanding, and short-tempered. They will make quick, bold,

Chapter 10: Personality and Behavior

and reckless decisions. When they do not get their way, get ready for the fireworks. They helped coin the phrase, *"If you can't take the heat, get out of the kitchen!"*

Influence-I tends to gossip and exaggerate. Sarcasm and trash-talking come easy. They take shortcuts and rely on their ability to talk their way out of any trouble. They will lack follow-through and rarely finish what they begin. Influence-I's are known for smooth talking, to over promise and under deliver. They helped coin the phrase, *"It's getting deep in here!"*

Steady-S can become a victim when out of balance, a party pooper, a carrier of PLOM (poor little 'ole me) disease. They tend to take things very personal and can be too hard on themselves. Being a doormat and allowing people to walk on them comes easy. They will not stand up to people. They allow others to falsely think they agree with them. They are known to give up too easily. Steady-S's hold their feelings in and make people guess what they think or feel. They helped coin the phrase, *"Do you think I'm a mind reader?"*

Conscientious-C's still have their first dollar. They are nitpickers and too methodical. These folks get bogged down in details and wait for just the right conditions before taking action. They can be very judgmental and a perfectionist. They will sit back and wait for others to make mistakes to avoid taking blame. They can be pessimistic and negative. Conscientious C's do not like to admit when they are wrong. They helped coin the phrase, *"It's hard to be humble when you're perfect in every way."*

Balancing Our Strengths

When we are balanced and taking advantage of our personality we can see that each and every one of us has so much to offer.

Dominant-D You enjoy solving problems, getting things done, and achieving goals. You are a natural leader and enjoy being in charge. You have high standards for performance. You trust your ability to produce results. You are able to make decisions quickly. You enjoy challenges and competition. You are willing to take risks and leap out above the crowd. You get over things very quickly.

Influence-I You are optimistic, charming, and outgoing. You genuinely like people. You trust people and enjoy bringing out their best. You are a strong communicator. You enjoy telling stories. You enjoy meeting new people, working with others, and networking. You motivate and inspire people. You never meet a stranger. You are usually happy and see the big picture of life. You are a dreamer and visionary.

Steady-S You are loyal, sympathetic, and supportive. You are a good listener and a team-player. You enjoy helping people. You are steady and consistent. You respect the way things are done. You are very cooperative. You put effort into being harmonious and stable. You do not need to be in the limelight. You are a peacemaker and very patient. You stick with a project from beginning to completion.

Conscientious-C You are accurate and logical. You do your homework before making a decision. You are precise and can be taken for face value. You have great attention to details. You are organized and have great time management skills. You are excellent at creating systems and methods. You are compliant and able to work alone. You have very high standards and produce quality results.

Summary

Points to ponder-

Personality is a flexible but predictive pattern.

We are capable of most behaviors under certain situations.

Weakness can be the results of a vacuum caused by over using strengths.

All of us have strengths that are valuable

What would a winner do?

Ask others how they view my personality and take notes.

Know, in detail, the personalities of those closest to me.

Focus on what I do have (strengths) and keep them in balance.

Chapter 11
Applying Personality

If we cannot end our differences, at least we can make the world safe for diversity – John F. Kennedy, Thirty-fifth President of the USA

In this chapter I have listed some specific areas of life and how they apply to each personality type. Some of these traits have already been mentioned. They have been listed again when applicable to the particular topic. This is a great area of the book to keep handy as a reference tool because many of these are experienced daily.

When Parenting

Dominant-D, Principal - authoritative and enforces the rules

Influence-I, Friend - fun and games

Steady-S, Teacher - caregiver and instructional

Conscientious-C, Evaluator - observes and studies

In Relationships

Dominant-D, acts as a leader – takes charge

Influence-I, acts as an inspirer – cheerleader and encourager

Steady-S, acts as a coach – supports and instructs

Conscientious-C, acts as an examiner – questions and analyzes

How to Recognize

Dominant-D, they tend to be active, and always in a rush. They speak loudly and come right to the point in conversation. They like to take charge of meetings, set the agenda, and make the rules. They can be aggressive, blunt, and impatient.

Influence-I, they tend to be outgoing, friendly, and charming. They speak using gestures and facial expressions, tell stories, and laugh. They like to make gatherings (meetings and sales presentations) into social events. They enjoy working with people, often trying to include others in their projects.

Steady-S, they tend to be quiet, indirect, and casual. They do not show their emotions. They speak slowly and in a relaxed pace, as if they have nowhere important to go. They are good listeners. They encourage others to talk about themselves. They prefer to follow, not to lead. They like working with others in small groups.

Conscientious-C, they tend to be quiet, indirect, and formal. They appear cautious. They speak slowly and factual. They try to use proper grammar. They rarely speak up at meetings. When they do, it's accurate and intelligent. They prefer to go off by themselves and to collect data and make plans. Their offices are neat.

Communicating in Style

When relating with others this information can be a godsend. The following is useful when communicating or working with others.

Dominant-D, Be ready to present your requirements without wasting their time. Be clear, specific, and to the point. Involve them in developing a solution. Let them decide how to accomplish it and give them the freedom to do it by themselves. Be firm and stand up to them. Focus on the facts and results.

Influence-I, Be friendly and visit in a personable way before getting down to business. Help them set clear, realistic goals. Develop time frames and check back with them frequently. Maintain an open door policy with them. Make them feel included. Look for ways to make the best use of their verbal skills.

Steady-S, Be kind and relaxed. Briefly catch up before getting down to business. Notify them in advance about future changes so they can adjust. Show interest and support for them. Allow them to work behind the scenes. Encourage them to speak up at meetings.

Conscientious-C, Do not beat around the bush, get right down to business. Present the facts and focus on the issues at hand. Involve them in creating systems and developing procedures. Ask their opinions and wait for them to answer. Involve them in long term planning. Respect their personal limits. Do not mix them with too many people, too long.

What Turns You Off

Dominant-D

- Small talk or chitchat
- Wasting their time
- Telling them what to do
- Expecting them to do what you tell them to do
- Not telling them what is on your mind
- Trying to control them

Influence-I

- Boring them with details
- Having to be quiet too long
- Making them feel like an outsider
- Being negative around them
- Isolating them away from people
- Expecting them to follow a rigid schedule

Steady-S
- Popping changes on them
- Confronting or personally attacking them
- Rushing or expecting them to move quickly
- Questioning their loyalty
- Surrounding them with hostility
- Forcing them to debate or argue

Conscientious-C
- Yelling at them
- Demanding or proving they are wrong
- Giving them a mission with no plan
- Making them the center of attention
- Insisting they be more positive
- Surrounding them with lots of people, often

What Motivates You

Dominant-D
- Primary motivation - results
- Working in a fast-paced environment
- Being in charge
- Taking on new opportunities
- Solving problems
- Always having room for advancement in your career

Chapter 11: Applying Personality

Influence-I

- Primary motivation - people
- Being in the spotlight (not necessarily being in charge)
- Tackling new projects and learning new things
- Gaining public recognition
- Variety and change
- Telling stories or jokes

Steady-S

- Primary motivation - cooperation
- Working in a stable environment
- Working on one task at a time
- Being recognized for your loyalty and service
- Having clear and unchanging rules
- Working with a small group of people where you can develop relationships

Conscientious–C

- Primary motivation – quality
- Being smart and knowledgeable
- Having access to information and data
- Having time to work a plan to completion
- Being dealt with in a formal manner
- Being recognized and rewarded for specific accomplishments
- Organized and clean environments

Part III: I Give on the Outside

Camping in Style

Four families go on a camping trip. Each family has a different primary personality style. The group consists of Dominant Dave, Influence Ida, Steady Steve, and Conscientious Cathy. The big day has finally arrived.

The alarm clock goes off and Dominant Dave immediately turns it off, jumps out of bed, and he's off and running. Influence Ida reaches over and hits the snooze button because she figures she can make up for the nine minutes later. Steady Steve turns off the clock, peels back the covers, then slowly but steadily gets out of bed. Conscientious Cathy hits her snooze button because she has already preset her clock ahead to compensate for the nine minute loss.

Dominant Dave is brushing his teeth with an electric toothbrush because a manual toothbrush is too slow. Influence Ida has hit her snooze button one more time because she is convinced she can make up the time later. Steady Steve is making coffee so it will be available when his wife gets up. Conscientious Cathy enjoys a cup of coffee that was automatically made before she woke up.

Dominant Dave gathers all of his family together and gives each member a list of what to bring to the vehicle, while he loads it the way he wants it loaded. Influence Ida is in the shower and has not even thought about what she is taking camping. Steady Steve has been loading his vehicle, here and there, for the last two weeks and is almost done. Conscientious Cathy loaded her vehicle last night as soon as she got home from the "How to make the best out of your camping trip" seminar.

They have all agreed to meet for breakfast. Dominant Dave will be the first one there because he is speeding, as usual. He darts in and out of traffic and wants to get there in the shortest amount of time. Influence Ida is all over the road, driving fast, slow, and then fast again. She has been pulled over for not paying attention because she was talking *and* looking at her husband while driving. She talks the police officer out of a ticket. Steady Steve is in the right lane and driving slow, as usual. He has traffic backed up behind him and has already been honked at three times for not going as soon as the light turned green. Conscientious Cathy has stopped to get fuel. She kept

Chapter 11: Applying Personality

her receipt, recorded it in her checkbook, and recorded her mileage in the log book. She just looked at her roadmap for the third time this morning.

At breakfast, Dominant Dave orders the same thing every time. He swallows his food almost whole and rather quickly. Influence Ida is the last one to order because she is too busy talking. She eventually eats everything in sight. Steady Steve eats deliberate and slow. He rarely gains weight. Influence Ida thinks he is lucky. Conscientious Cathy is a picky eater and knows all the combo specials.

They arrive at the campgrounds to settle in. Dominant Dave is simply using a sleeping bag, roughing it under the stars. Influence Ida has gotten a cabin with upgrades - water, electricity, and internet connection. Steady Steve is staying with the families of Influence Ida and Conscientious Cathy so he can help with extras. Conscientious Cathy is staying in her new RV. The one she purchased last night at the "How to make the most out of your camping trip" seminar. Influence Ida was the one who held the seminar and sold her the RV.

For survival tools, Influence Ida has brought her laptop, portable TV, and video camera. Steady Steve has extra toilet paper, toothbrushes, and soap in case anyone runs out. Conscientious Cathy has a compass, GPS, and a set of walkie talkies. Dominant Dave simply brings his Crocodile Dundee, extra large, pocket knife.

Dominant Dave is making a fire when all of a sudden a grizzly bear approaches. He firmly stands up and attempts to face off with the bear. Influence Ida grabs her video camera because she is convinced this will be a great hit on youtube.com. Steady Steve tries to talk Dominant Dave out of fighting, as he himself is running away! Conscientious Cathy is so pleased with the responses of everyone that she quickly removes the fake bear costume and congratulates them for passing her drill. She was also afraid of getting cut by Dominant Dave's pocket knife.

They all turn in and say their prayers. Dominant Dave thanks God for helping him accomplish all of his goals for the day and asks God for more patience. Influence Ida thanks God for the video footage and promises, one more time, to stop procrastinating, starting tomorrow. Steady Steve prays for all of the different family members, individually. Then he asks God for more courage to say what is on his mind. Conscientious Cathy has asked God for more peace and less anxiety for all the problems she thinks could happen. Then she asks God to help her be more optimistic.

Did you notice how the families used their specific strengths which covered the weakness of each other? Or how they used their individual strengths to get the same job done in different ways? Psychologist and founder of Smalley Family Institute, Dr. Gary Smalley says, "*If two people are just alike then one isn't needed.*" It is so true, and once we realize it our differences no longer cripple us, they empower us!

I have some personal friends, Randy and Debbie Lipp, who love camping. They have four sons (poor Debbie), and their family has been going camping as long as I have known them. If there is ever a place where things can go wrong, it is camping. Yet, there is a bond that is evident among the Lipp family. They have learned, through diversity in camping, how to appreciate the individual strengths that each member contributes.

This concludes the personality portion, for now. Towards the end of the book I have enclosed a personality chart in the *gauging* section. It is a detailed list of the strengths we covered, by each personality style. You can use it to create a report that will identify, track, and improve upon your specific strengths and needs. It also helps you specifically identify the strengths and needs of others.

Summary

Points to ponder –

Personality is unique and valuable when understood.

The more we understand about personality the better we relate and communicate.

Differences can be very valuable when understood.

Understanding personality is an important part of teamwork.

What would a winner do?

Appreciate the differences in each other.

Instead of weaknesses, focus on the strengths of myself and others.

Chapter 12
Winning - On Purpose

Here is the test to find whether your mission on earth is finished. If you're alive, it isn't. - Richard Bach, American Author

In the Army they used to tell us to move with a purpose – not just halfheartedly but with a purpose. I believe your purpose, at whatever you do, is the fuel that will burn when all other fuels seem dry. If you have a pulse, you have a purpose. Are you making a living or making a difference?

Lee Iacocca certainly made a great living by rising to the top of the corporate ladder. Iacocca was best known for his role as CEO of Chrysler. He wrote a book called *Straight Talk*. In it he said, *"Here I am in the twilight of my life, still wondering what it's all about. I can tell you this, fame and fortune is for the birds."*

Perhaps you have asked, "What is my purpose in life, Why am I here? What was I created for?" It seems like the only type of people who ask those questions are typically folks who...breathe. We are not alone in wanting to know our purpose. Trying to learn what it is can be quite difficult and troublesome. However, once you finally discover your purpose it is extremely rewarding.

I have a good friend who battles depression and one reason is because he simply cannot figure out his purpose in life. Do you know anyone like this? I wrote this poem for those of us who may ever wonder *"What good am I?"*

What Good Am I

Love is a human desire, right from the start; we do unusual things to fill this void in our heart.

Some use vices such as people, power, sex, or health; while others use work, food, drugs, or wealth.

All of those leave you longing for more, regardless of whether you're rich or poor.

If longing for more were the only real price then it would be easy, just find a new vice.

The real pain comes from the false impression that you can find love in an outer possession.

The more you're let down the less you may believe that you were created in the image of the King.

How could a God who's supposed to be love let this happen if he sees all from above?

He allows you to choose because love doesn't force; He gave you free will so you could have a choice.

He's the only source that will never let you down; continue trusting in Him to keep true love around.

Sometimes it's a challenge to know what you're worth; but God had a perfect plan for you, even before your birth.

In case you ever question, "What good am I?"

You're one of the reasons that Jesus came to die!

Try to remember the next time you're feeling blue, the world has a specific need that can only be filled by you.

The Purpose of Life

There are many different views concerning the purpose of life. We hear of things such as: to love, serve, give, worship God, to nurture, or pro-create. A step to finding your purpose is to know you were created to be a giver. We have discussed many different areas of giving. But when it comes to fulfilling your purpose, giving should be the foundation. How do we know this? Giving is a sure way to fulfill your desire for love.

The steps look like this;

> Our *desire for love* is fulfilled by *giving love* which is fulfilled by *meeting the needs of others*.

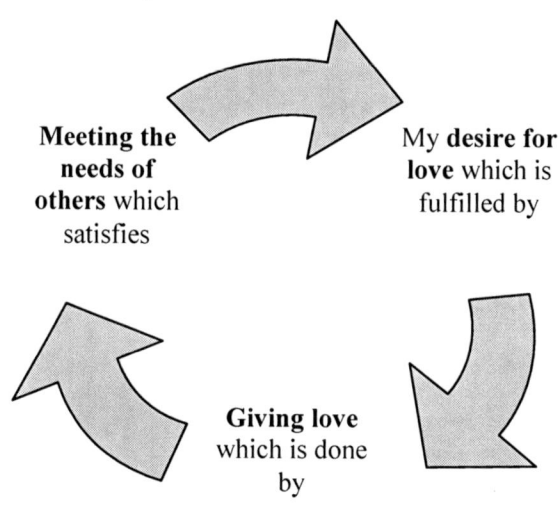

Meeting the needs of others which satisfies

My desire for love which is fulfilled by

Giving love which is done by

You were created to fill the needs of others. Is that not what a giver does? As a matter of fact, if the world did not have needs, none of us would be *needed!* Have you ever known someone who was a very hard worker yet they did not seem to be where they wanted to be in life? Or someone who was extremely smart but did not seem to be where they wanted to be? Although hard work, intelligence, and many other factors are important, our full potential is recognized by how well we fill the needs of others. One of my favorite quotes from Ziglar is, *"You can have everything in life you want if you will just help enough other people get what they want."*

Filling the Needs of Others

In the most basic way, you and I meet needs daily simply by existing. Our very survival and existence requires the use of things like food, clothing, and shelter. When we purchase and use those items, we directly and indirectly meet the needs of suppliers, salespeople, manufactures, and many others. Your labor provides a service or product for people. It gives jobs to accountants, attorneys, and payroll companies. It helps support the government and creates opportunity. Opening doors, giving smiles, and hugging someone are all ways to fill needs. You also fill needs for your family, friends, co-workers, strangers, animals, and the environment. You can meet needs through parenting, grand parenting, fathering, mothering, or friendships. The list goes on. What may seem insignificant to you and me can mean a tremendous difference to others. You meet more needs in a day than you likely imagine. Therefore, you are being a giver. Even in the Bible, there are over six hundred commandments and laws. Yet when the master of giving, Jesus himself, came, He summed all of them down to just two.

- Love the Lord your God with all your heart, mind, body, and soul. Could this mean *grow on the inside?*
- Love your neighbor as yourself. Could this mean *give on the outside?*

The Wrong Place at the Right Time

Have you ever met someone who says they love what they do in life, and they *really* do? What makes them so special? It is likely because they are doing what they were made to do. Not because they are any better at giving.

Considering there are so many ways to meet needs it can be quite difficult to put our finger on our *specific* purpose in life. Maybe you have already discovered yours. If you have, you are part of a very rare group. If you are still searching, the personality section should have gotten your wheels spinning. It is one of the first tools you can use in your pursuit.

> "The goal is to fit a career to our purpose rather than fitting our purpose to a career."

Let's look at careers for a moment. Rarely will a person pursue their first job based on their purpose. Upon entering adulthood, many people take jobs as a means to survival. Others take jobs as a tool to assist in acquiring more of the wishlist. With these motives, we often end up taking jobs with *receiving* in mind, not *giving*. In many cases, the primary reason for the job has nothing to do with our purpose but everything to do with the proceeds. The job simply ends up being the wrong place at the right time. Very few end up staying in those jobs forever. Among the ones who do stay, fewer end up finding their purpose in that initial job. I am not suggesting this is wrong. However, I am suggesting it is reality. Typically, a career is not where we find our purpose. A career is simply an area of life that allows us to be compensated for meeting needs. The goal is to fit a career to our purpose rather than fitting our purpose to a career. We should want to spend time on and off the job fulfilling our purpose. Dr. Howard Hendricks says, "Your career is what you are paid for and your calling is what you are made for."

The Elite 20%

Marcus Buckingham, past Sr. Researcher of The Gallup Organization, says Gallup did a poll in the early 2000's. Over two million people completed a personality profile which identified their specific strengths. They were then asked the following question. *Do you spend most of your day working from your strengths?* Only 20% answered "yes." Are you kidding me? 80% polled were not working from their strengths, **eighty percent**! No wonder people are so unmotivated and edgy.

We are a world full of stress, all desiring to win, and we keep hearing (like this book) that we must give, give, and give. Yet, most of us are swimming upstream and find it very difficult to *give* effectively. If you are one of those 80 percent I highly encourage you to apply the personality section we covered earlier. I hope you will read it a few times. It will expose new insight every time.

Could you imagine taking a hammer into the shower with you? Or wearing a catcher's mitt while you tie your shoes? Of course not, that's not where they belong. They are made for other areas of life. I don't know if you have a dominant or steady personality. I do know you have specific qualities, traits, and characteristics within yourself that make great sense in some areas of life and no sense in others. Orison Swett Marden, founder of Success Magazine, says, *"No man can be ideally successful until he has found his place. Like a locomotive, he is strong on the track but weak anywhere else."* Me personally, I have no business in an administrative position - of any kind. Places that involve tiny details – not for me, not for long!

I have a friend, Velvet Torres, who helped edit this book. She actually inspired me to go ahead and get started on the writing when I did. I was concerned about the style, editing, grammar, and punctuation. She showed me a way that I could do what I'm good at and let someone else help me with the areas where I have no business being. Had I tried to be in all areas, I would not have been proactive. The more time we spend in proper areas specific to us, the more effective we are.

I just used a silly analogy about taking a hammer in the shower. At least the hammer was laying neutral and not being used outside of its strength. With 80% of us working *away* from our strengths, it would be like trying to use the hammer as a washcloth. Ouch! When we are trying day in and day out to work outside of our strengths, it is literally painful.

Looking for Your Purpose

There was a man who finally found his purpose in life. He also learned to delegate in areas where he wasn't strong. He was in the barber shop sharing his new ideas with the others. He was really excited because he had just hired a *professional worrier.* He claimed he was able to take all his worries, stresses, overdue bills, and other problems downtown and turn them over to this new expert. His barber asked him how much this amazing service cost him. *"$1,000 per day,"* said the man, in a peaceful tone. *"Wow, $1000 per day? You can't afford that!"* said the barber. *"Yeah, I know I can't, let him worry about it!"* replied the man.

Please take the time to answer the following questions. It will likely take some serious thinking to answer all of them. But knowing one's purpose is a part of life that should take serious thinking. Ask yourself:

If I were a tool, which one would keep me in a *giving* mode the most often? The reality is, in a sense you and I are a tool (I hope you are not still thinking about that hammer!) You are a very effective tool when doing what you were created to do. Would you be a tool

Chapter 12: Winning on Purpose

that helps fix people physically, mentally, or spiritually? Tools like doctors, preachers, counselors, or nurses? Would you be a tool that helps protect people, such as a police officer or fireman? How about an educator, teacher, speaker, lecturer, or professor? You could be a tool used for delivering, assembling, analyzing, calculating, building, managing, or comforting.

Imagine next week is *do-anything, be-anybody week*. Everybody has agreed to allow anyone to tag along with them for the week. Who would you tag along with? Or who would you want to tag along with you? Qualification does not matter. Would it be a pilot, preacher, or student? How about a housewife, driver, or dog-trainer?

Forget all the obstacles or fears that can cloud your thoughts. We will cover them later. Let your mind go free. Say to yourself, *"I am very effective when I am doing _____."* Will you write them down right now? It could make a huge difference in your life.

I am very effective, happy, productive, joyful, or kind when I:

If you have not identified your specific purpose in life, I encourage you to participate in this. *Right now* is one of those times in life that you talked about yesterday and labeled it as *later*. Have you ever said *"I will do it later?"* Later has now arrived. ☺

> Hi, my name is *later*. I arrived sooner than you expected but I am actually on time. Let's take action now!

I encourage you to fill in the above list as you think of other areas or ideas throughout the week.

What do you daydream about? Keep this book handy so when you catch yourself daydreaming, you can write down the details.

Where do you see yourself at the end of this life? Start with the future in mind. Do you believe you go to heaven, to hell, in the ground, somewhere else, or reincarnated? This has major significance in your purpose. Just as you use a roadmap, you need to know where you are right now *and* where you are headed. Then and only then are you able to take the appropriate route.

Ask yourself what you are good at or what you enjoy? You have specific skills that you do very well. Things you really enjoy. When you are doing them you find yourself losing track of time.

Ask your friends what you are good at. Often times your true friends can give you an honest perception that you, yourself, may never see.

What would you do if you had plenty of money? If you woke up tomorrow with so much money you had to hire someone just to manage the interest, what would you do with your time? Okay, I mean after the initial three or six months of traveling and buying everything under the sun!

What can you do with your hands tied behind your back? Things that make every one envy you. You make it look so easy and natural.

What interests you, big time? What fascinates you? What is it that consumes your thoughts so much that you lose focus on what you're supposed to be doing? What do you think about the most?

What or where do you spend most of your time and money? As we discussed in the beginning, your checkbook and calendar is a great way to see the inside of your heart.

If you haven't written something down, I want to encourage you again to do it now. As stated earlier, tomorrow is one of the greatest labor-saving devices ever invented. Once you have identified possible areas that fit your purpose, ask yourself these qualifying questions.

By doing this, will I be serving others and filling their needs? Will I be giving love? Your proposed purpose *must* meet both of these qualifications or it is far from being your purpose. Or anyone else's for that matter.

Summary

Points to ponder-

You have a specific purpose that can only be fulfilled by you.

Your purpose will usually involve giving from your strengths.

What would a winner do?

Pay the price to discover and live for my purpose - it's worth it!

Part IV: I Gain From My Pain

Chapter 13
Purpose, Problems, and Pain

Every winner has scars – Herbert N. Casson, American Author

Now that you have some general direction as to what makes your heart tick, you can plunge deeper into learning about your purpose.

I am absolutely convinced that pain is the main separator between poor and rich, fear and love, or losers and winners. That is a bold claim but I believe it with all my heart. Do you remember in the introduction of this book when I asked *If winning is so wonderful, why do we not have more winners in life?* Most of us can shine, perform, maintain, and "hold our own" when things are going well. However, when too much pain enters the picture, a separation takes place. Winners are willing, or able, to put forth the effort needed to manage and *gain* from the pain.

> "If pain does not come before pleasure, it will likely come afterwards."

Can we really gain from pain? Thirst is what makes water valuable. Sinking makes rising valuable. Loss is what makes gain valuable. The *pain* in all of them is what makes the *pleasure* in all of them valuable. We would never appreciate the value of pleasure without knowing the lack of pleasure (pain).

Pain causes a needed pressure when traveling the winner's highway. Like the tires on your vehicle, too much pressure can result in a rough ride. Too little pressure results in poor performance. Surprisingly, many people identify their specific purpose in the very last place they would ever expect, in a place that is not welcomed. A place most of us want to avoid called *pain*. There is a lot of purpose buried within our problems and pain. Pain is a major factor in fulfilling pleasure. If pain does not come before pleasure, it will likely come afterwards.

Fighting on Behalf of Children

July 27, 2006, will go down in history as the day that changed how America protects its children from sexual predators. At a ceremony in the Rose Garden, President George W. Bush signed a new, tough-as-nails law[12]. One to track and apprehend convicted sex offenders who disappear after their release from prison. The date was not chosen randomly. It was exactly 25 years earlier that John Walsh and his wife Revé suffered the most horrendous loss that any parent could endure. It was the abduction and murder of their six-year-old son, Adam. Since that day in 1981, John has dedicated himself to fighting on behalf of children and all crime victims. As a result, thousands of victims have found justice. And many abducted children have been safely brought home. The new law signed by President Bush is also a result of John's fight. It's called "The Adam Walsh Child Protection and Safety Act."

Most people know Walsh as the dedicated host of "America's Most Wanted" (www.amw.com), the man whose groundbreaking television program has helped take down nearly 1,000 dangerous fugitives in the past 20 years. But it's not the career that he envisioned for himself. Walsh moved to Florida with his wife Revé and was living the American Dream. He was a successful businessman, building high-end luxury hotels and building his life. But after Adam's murder, everything changed.

If something happened to your child, God forbid, and you had to choose between John Walsh and me to find that child, who would it be? I expect you said Walsh. Is it because I don't care or that I could not help - of course not. Walsh is more qualified, has more of an interest, and is more passionate. Mainly because of the pain he experienced in his own life. Now, *because of that pain*, he has a huge purpose in life. He is giving love to others in a way that only he is able to give.

Chapter 13: Purpose, Problems, and Pain

They Saved Each Others Life

The following story was written by Rick Reilly in Sports Illustrated[13].

Strongest Dad in the World

I try to be a good father. Give my kids mulligans. Work nights to pay for their text messaging. Take them to swimsuit shoots - but compared with Dick Hoyt, not even close. Eighty-five times he's pushed his disabled son, Rick, 26.2 miles in marathons. Eight times he's not only pushed him 26.2 miles in a wheelchair but also towed him 2.4 miles in a dinghy while swimming and pedaled him 112 miles in a seat on the handlebars, all in the same day. Dick's also pulled him cross-country skiing, taken him on his back mountain climbing and once hauled him across the U.S. on a bike. Makes taking your son bowling look a little lame, right? And what has Rick done for his father? Not much, except save his life.

This love story began in Winchester, Mass., 43 years ago, when Rick was strangled by the umbilical cord during birth, leaving him brain-damaged and unable to control his limbs. "He'll be a vegetable the rest of his life," Dick says doctors told him and his wife, Judy, when Rick was nine months old. "Put him in an institution." But the Hoyts weren't buying it. They noticed the way Rick's eyes followed them around the room.

When Rick was 11 they took him to the engineering department at Tufts University and asked if there was anything to help the boy communicate. "No way," Dick says he was told. "There's nothing going on in his brain." "Tell him a joke," Dick countered. They did. Rick laughed. Turns out a lot was going on in his brain.

Rigged up with a computer that allowed him to control the cursor by touching a switch with the side of his head, Rick was finally able to communicate. First words? "Go Bruins!" After a high school classmate was paralyzed in an accident and the school organized a charity run for him, Rick pecked out, "Dad, I want to do that." Yeah, right. How was Dick, a self-described "porker" who never ran more than a mile at a time, going to push his son five miles? Still, he tried. "Then it was me who was handicapped," Dick says. "I was sore for two weeks." That day changed Rick's life. "Dad,"

Part IV: I Gain From My Pain

he typed, "when we were running, it felt like I wasn't disabled anymore!" And that sentence changed Dick's life.

He became obsessed with giving Rick that feeling as often as he could. He got into such hard-belly shape that he and Rick were ready to try the 1979 Boston Marathon. "No way," Dick was told by a race official. The Hoyts weren't quite a single runner, and they weren't quite a wheelchair competitor. For a few years Dick and Rick just joined the massive field and ran anyway, and then they found a way to get into the race officially.

In 1983 they ran another marathon so fast they made the qualifying time for Boston the following year. Then somebody said, "Hey, Dick, why not a triathlon?" How's a guy who never learned to swim and hadn't ridden a bike since he was six going to haul his 110-pound kid through a triathlon? Still, Dick tried. Now they've done 212 triathlons, including four grueling 15-hour Ironmans in Hawaii.

It must be a buzz-kill to be a 25-year-old stud getting passed by an old guy towing a grown man in a dinghy, don't you think? Hey, Dick, why not see how you'd do on your own? "No way," he says. Dick does it purely for "the awesome feeling" he gets from seeing Rick with a cantaloupe smile as they run, swim and ride together. This year, at ages 65 and 43, Dick and Rick finished their 24th Boston Marathon, in 5,083rd place out of more than 20,000 starters. Their best time, two hours, 40 minutes in 1992 - only 35 minutes off the world record, which, in case you don't keep track of these things, happens to be held by a guy who was not pushing another man in a wheelchair at the time.

"No question about it," Rick types. "My dad is the Father of the Century." And Dick got something else out of all this too. Two years ago he had a mild heart attack during a race. Doctors found that one of his arteries was 95% clogged. "If you hadn't been in such great shape," one doctor told him, "you probably would've died 15 years ago." So, in a way, Dick and Rick saved each other's life.

Rick, who has his own apartment (he gets home care) and works in Boston, and Dick, retired from the military and living in Holland, Mass., always find ways to be together. They give speeches around the country and compete in some backbreaking race every weekend, including this Father's Day. That night, Rick will buy his dad

Chapter 13: Purpose, Problems, and Pain

dinner, but the thing he really wants to give him is a gift he can never buy. "The thing I'd most like," Rick types, "is that my dad sit in the chair and I push him once."

I have worn out a box of tissues learning about these two amazing men. I encourage you to view their inspiring video here. www.iwasborntowin.com/videos/hoyt You will see a perfect example of purpose that came from tremendous pain.

Through Their Pain

James Robison was never raised by a father. He was born from a raped mother. When he was a teenager his father, the rapist, came back and tried to kill his mother. Robison nearly killed him in self defense[14]. Today, James and his wife, Betty, have a TV show, *Life Today*. James and Betty have helped touch the lives of millions, specifically parentless orphans. It's not how you start in life, it's how you finish.

You have likely heard of the national organization that has grown to over 600 affiliates and two million members and supporters. They have helped save nearly 300,000 lives through research-based programs[15]. Because of this organization, alcohol-related traffic deaths have decreased by 44 percent. This happened because two moms, Candace Lightner and Cindi Lamb, lost children to drunk drivers in 1980. They formed a group called MADD - Mothers Against Drunk Driving.

Passion from Pain

Personally, I now write, speak, and coach on personal growth. I have a huge passion for what I do. Mainly because of the huge amounts of pain I experienced as I was trying to find love in all the wrong places. My purpose is to share my experiences with other people. I no longer allow pain to use or control me. Rather, I use the pain from my worst to help me love and bring out the best in others. A *test*imony only comes after the "test." Do you have one? It will tell you a lot about what God has done for you and what he wants you to do for him!

Part IV: I Gain From My Pain

Although my purpose was finally revealed, I still had plenty of work left. My problems were not solved immediately. Learning my purpose helped motivate me to learn more about my problems and to look for solutions. As I learned more and became more peaceful, my passion increased tremendously.

Passion after the Pain

Passion usually comes after problems and pain. This is how life works a lot of the time. Think about it for a moment. We are most passionate about things that have relieved us of our biggest problems and pain. If you are having challenges in a certain area there is a great chance you will be used later to help someone else with that same challenge. What are some major problems at this moment of your life? Do any of these apply to you?

Money	Jobs	Organization	Focus	Children
Parenting	Overweight	Underweight	Relationships	Forgiveness
Health	Commitment	Spirituality	Behavior	Anger
Image	Alcohol	Drugs	Motivation	Bad habits

When it comes to problems in life we could make the list as large as time would allow. Do you know anyone who spends their life helping people with the problems we listed above? This makes a very important point. *Every problem is also a purpose!* A weight problem for one person is another person's purpose to help people with weight problems. A drug problem for one is a purpose for someone else to help people with drugs. Do you see how they go hand in hand? Who better to help than the one who has experienced and overcome the same challenge?

Experiencing the pain before the solution is a huge motivation towards passion. Knowing what brought about the pain, how it could have been avoided, and how to overcome it is what helps others down the road. I realize some solutions can come from a textbook. But when it gets down to the trenches of life a textbook is only an assistant. You and I are in the school of life and we should want to learn how to fix broken hearts. The best way to learn is from our own experiences. As you know, the world is full of broken hearts and your services are in great need. You might be surprised at how passionate you will become at solving some of your biggest challenges, once you start looking for purpose within the pain. Thomas Jefferson said it quite well, "Who then can so softly bind up the wound of another as he who has felt the same wound himself."

Summary

Points to ponder-

Problems ultimately create passion

Pain ignites passion

Pain exposes purpose

What would a winner do?

Look for my purpose within my greatest pain.

Chapter 14
Pain for the Proper Purpose is Productive

I conceive that pleasures are to be avoided if greater pains be the consequence, and pains to be coveted that will terminate in greater pleasures. - Michel Eyquem De Montaigne, French Writer

By actively looking for a proper purpose within our pain we will be more apt to understand and face it. We can also learn to effectively distinguish between useless pain and proper pain. Here is a little tongue-twisting, humor about pain.

Pain for the Proper Purpose is Productive

Perhaps it's primarily my perception, but to be a proactive prospect we must ponder the positive possibilities of prospering without permitting the past and present to postpone the process. Pain from the past will attempt to be a perpetrator that promotes pity and poverty instead of profit. It prompts us to paint poor pictures of people, particularly our own inner portrait.

In place of preserving the privilege to protest, I prefer to persuade you to participate in the parade of life; which proudly proclaims that pain for the proper purpose is productive, powerful, and probable. Presuming this as a prerequisite provides you with proper preparation, passion, perseverance, and patience. This plan propels you to persist on a powerful path in pursuit of your purpose. It precludes many preventable problems like pride, prejudice, and procrastination.

Politicians, presidents, preachers, pastors, painters, policeman, and plenty of other people have fallen prey to this popular paralyzing prowler portrayed as pain. This potent, perspiring, phobia is predictable if you position yourself to penetrate and prune it with pliers of premeditation and prioritizing. A popular and prominent passage promises that praying for the presence of God has proven to be protective and pleasurable. This payback is a profound proverbial prize worth a pretty penny from the Prince of Peace. Now, how do you like them papples? ☺

I hope you got a little kick out of the paragraph. Laughter is so important, especially when it helps us gain from pain.

The ultimate measure of a man is not where he stands in moments of comfort and convenience, but where he stands at times of challenge and controversy. - Martin Luther King, Jr.

Why Does God Allow Pain in Our Life

In the early morning hours of Dec. 22, 2005, head coach of the Indianapolis Colts, Tony Dungy, and his wife Lauren, lived a parent's worst nightmare. They learned their eldest son and second of five children, 18-year-old James, had been found dead in his apartment. James' death was determined a suicide. Just six weeks after, on Saturday February 4, Dungy spoke at the Super Bowl Breakfast in Detroit, at the Marriott Renaissance Center. Dungy said he had learned a lot from his sons, Eric, 14 and Jordan, 5, *"but the most important thing came from James, who would have been 19,"* Dungy said.

He went on to make one of the most amazing speeches about pain. Here is a man who had just gone through pain that I can not even fathom. I hope his message enlightens you like it has me.

I'm going to illustrate three things that I've learned about the Lord, and I'm going to use my boys to illustrate that. I'm going to start with my middle son, Eric. He's 14 years old, and if you watch a lot of football, you've probably seen him on the sidelines of Colts games. He looks more like me than my other two boys do. As a matter of fact, he looks so much like me, when I look at him I see myself at 14, and I see a lot of the same things. Eric is very competitive, ultra competitive. He is focused on sports to where it's almost a problem. He's super-emotional where it's almost scary. Now, those of you that see me now would say, "Wait a minute, that doesn't sound a lot like you," but it was me at 14. I grew up not too far from here in Jackson,

Chapter 14: Pain for the Proper Purpose is Productive

Michigan. There are some people in this room that knew me when I was 14 years old. So when I look at Eric now at 14, and I look at myself, that's one of the things I know about God. I know how powerful His Spirit is; I know that He can change people. I know that He'll do that if we allow Him to. And I really believe He's going to do that with Eric as he grows.

The second way I've seen God's hands at work is through our youngest son, Jordan. He's five years old. Jordan was born with a rare, very rare neurological condition. It's called congenital insensitivity to pain. There are only two or three cases in the whole United States. It's a little more prevalent in other countries, but there's only been about three diagnosed in the United States. Basically what happens, he is missing the conductors that allow the nerve signals to go from his body to his brain. And that sounds like it's good at the beginning, but, I promise you, it's not. We've learned a lot about pain in the last five years since we've had Jordan, and we've learned that some hurts are really necessary for kids.

Pain is necessary, really, for kids to find out the difference between what's good and what's harmful. Jordan loves cookies, but in his mind, if they're good out on the plate, they're even better in the oven. So he will go right in the oven if my wife's not looking when she's baking them. He'll reach in, take the rack out, take the pan out, burn his hands, okay, eat the cookie that's too hot, burn his tongue, and never feel it. And he doesn't know that it's bad for him. When we go to the park, he'll go on the slide, and all kids know it's fun to go up the slide and slide down. He has fun doing that, too. To him, it's just as much fun jumping off from the top. He has no fear of anything, so we constantly have to watch him.

We've also learned that pain actually helps the body heal. Something I didn't know until talking with the doctors. You get an injury, your brain senses there is pain there, and it sends the right healing agents naturally to that spot because it senses something is wrong. Without that sensation of feeling something is wrong, Jordan's body doesn't send those healing agents. Consequently, he's got cuts from June and July that haven't healed yet. So that's what we've seen.

Why does the Lord allow pain in your life? Why do bad things happen to good people? If God is a God of love, why does He allow these

Reader input: www.iwasborntowin.com/readerinput

Part IV: I Gain From My Pain

hurtful things to happen? Well, we've learned that, a lot of times, because of that pain, that little temporary pain, you learn what's harmful. You learn to fear the right things. Pain sometimes lets us know we've got a condition that needs to be healed, and pain inside sometimes lets us know that spiritually we are not quite right. We need to be healed, and God will send that healing agent right to the spot. And sometimes pain is the only way that will turn us, as kids, back to the Father. So we've learned a lot about that.

But I think the most important lesson that I've learned about the Lord, I learned from my oldest son, James. As you heard, James would have been 19, but he died right before Christmas. James was a Christian, and he was, by far, the most sensitive, the most compassionate, of all our boys; very, very compassionate, very sensitive.

As most teenage boys today, James was getting a lot of messages from the world that maybe that's not the way to be. You've all seen them on TV, in the movies, the music they listen to, the magazines that they are able to read. And you get those conflicting signals and mixed signals. And he was struggling very much with how you should respond to the world, and he ended up taking his life right before Christmas, and it was tough. It was very, very painful. But as painful as it was, there were some good things that came out of it.

When I was at the funeral, I talked about one of my biggest regrets, and it goes right along with the last thing that Bart just shared. James was home for Thanksgiving and was leaving, going back to school and going back to work, just the normal process. You don't think about it. I said, "Hey, I'll see you later." My daughter took him to the airport, we just exchanged, "See you later," and that was the last time I saw him. I talked to him on the phone a lot but never saw him again.

I shared at the funeral that my biggest regret was that I didn't give him a big hug the very last time I saw him. I met a guy the next day after the funeral, and he said, "You know, I was there, I heard you talking, I took off work today. I called my son, and I said, 'I'm going to take you to the movies, and we are going to spend some time and go to dinner.'" That was a real, real blessing to me. I've gotten a lot of letters like that from people who have heard what I said and said,

Chapter 14: Pain for the Proper Purpose is Productive

"Hey, you brought me a little closer to my son," or *"a little closer to my daughter,"* and that is a tremendous blessing.

We are able to donate some of James's organs to organ donors programs. Got a letter back about two weeks ago that two people had received his corneas and now can see. That has been a tremendous blessing. I had the privilege of talking to a young man who is James's age who was going through some struggles. Didn't know if he could make it, and we talked for about a week, and his voice just didn't sound good. But every day it sounded a little bit better and better, and about 10 days later he called me back and asked me how I was doing. I could just feel in his voice he was doing better, and he was going to make it, and that was a tremendous blessing.

It is interesting how we can see pain in a good way and gain from it rather than run from it. I have concluded Dungy's story in the last chapter of the book due to relevance.

Failing is Part of Winning

The easiest way to spot useless failure is when you see no failure at all. Failing can be very painful, especially if we don't focus on the purpose. We can actually train ourselves to appreciate failing when we know it is moving us forward. I deleted four times as many words from this book than are printed. I had to go through a lot of ways of learning what would not fit prior to realizing what worked. I did not fail; I simply went through a process.

Thomas Edison said he learned 10,000 ways he could not make a light bulb work. Each time took him closer to inventing the light bulb. Here is a side note that you may not be aware of. Interestingly enough, when he finally invented the light bulb, it was late at night. His wife said "Tom, turn out that light and come on to bed!"

Failing is part of winning, provided it is for the purpose of growing or giving. Because of his failure to keep a firm grip, Charles Goodyear mistakenly dropped rubber on his stove in the early 1800's. He found that heat made the rubber stronger. This is how Goodyear tires were invented. Investors who never lose money will rarely gain much. The best salespeople will hear more people say *no* than *yes*. The American

Philosopher, Elbert Hubbard, said "the greatest mistake a man can make is to be afraid of making one."

Good Pain vs. Bad Pain

Avoiding pain is wonderful and crucial if there really is no proper purpose. No sane person wants pain for nothing. We need to be able to identify when there is a purpose that is bigger than the pain. In other words, we want to separate the good pain from the bad pain. Avoiding good pain detours us from the winner's highways and sends us down roads full of useless pain and heartache. Then we take more detours. Unfortunately, unless we learn to face the good pain we just end up going in circles.

Good pain is what your mother went through in order for you to be born. Good pain is when you study hard for the passing grade. It is staying up all night with a newborn. Or when the single parent works three jobs and gives all he or she has for the children. Good pain is when Jesus Christ died on the cross for you and me. He certainly had a proper purpose in his pain; therefore it became part of the process.

Pain is Part of the Process

It was February 11, 1990, in Tokyo, Japan, far away from his American home of Ohio. At the young age of twenty-nine he would face one of his biggest battles ever. It was a major sporting event, a true David-and-Goliath story. His opponent had a winning record of 100 percent and was known for turning the strongest of men into helpless victims, most within minutes of the attack. He, on the other hand, had a reputation for running out of gas or not following through to completion. He was a tremendous underdog with odds of 42:1. It was predicted he would not last more than one and a half minutes. With odds and predictions like that, none of the major American media networks would even send reporters to Japan to cover the event.

To make matters worse, his mother unexpectedly died just three weeks prior. I think anyone would have understood had he chosen to cancel his appointment. Instead, he said his goal was to win this battle

Chapter 14: Pain for the Proper Purpose is Productive

for her. Not only did he make it past the 90 second mark, he surprisingly made it all the way to the eighth round where he would finally be knocked down. As he lay there on the canvas, the referee started counting, "one-two-three!" Ten seconds would confirm his predicted defeat if he did not get up soon. Time was flying, "six-seven-eight!" he heard, as the referee's hand continued to pound the floor. Although he had put up his best fight ever, the odds were now proving to be true. "Nine!" Then the referee's hand headed for the canvas one final time, the dreaded sound "ten!" was on its way to the fighter's ear. With milliseconds left and only inches between the referee's hand and the canvas, millions of people witnessed as a man with determination and desire stood to his feet.

In the tenth round he would make boxing history around the world. This was the night that a 42:1 underdog named James "Buster" Douglas would become the first person to ever send "Iron" Mike Tyson down to the canvas. Unlike "Buster," Tyson did not get up before the ten-count. James "Buster" Douglas became the new, undisputed, heavyweight champion of the world. He said his mom kept him in the ring and on his feet.

What made such a difference this one particular evening? He had a burning desire and a solid purpose. When your purpose is solid enough, pain is not avoided; it simply becomes part of the process.

Pain Promotes Positive Performance

When a person goes through an intervention it's because they have a problem so severe that someone from the outside has to intervene in their life. Pain is one of the crucial ingredients needed in order for the person to be willing to participate. The pain must be so great that the individual finally throws up their hands and surrenders to get help.

While bad pain drives us the wrong way in life, good pain promotes positive performance. This is why the cliché *I'm sick and tired of being sick and tired* is so popular. If you have an area of your life that you're sick of, ask yourself this. What does it do for me? Is it pain for the proper purpose? If it isn't, how does it hurt me? The more you focus on how bad it hurts you, the quicker you can start seeing the value of avoiding bad pain. The pain must be greater than the pleasure or we won't change. This is a rare moment when anger is good, not at you but the pain! Getting angry with yourself will not help you dig out of a hole. Getting angry with the pain of the problem will motivate change. Remember, pain is the motivation that usually drives us into bad situations. And pain can also motivate us to change our performance. I am not suggesting we focus on problems. I am, however, suggesting we focus on the *pain* from problems and use it to motivate us to find solutions.

Problem	What does it do for me?	How does it hurt me?
Yelling	Releases tension and stress.	Guilt, remorse, angry with self, feels out of control.
Unforgiving	Gives me control or makes me feel safe.	Bitterness, resentment, anger, hatred, or stress.
Alcohol/drug abuse	Relieves stress, tastes good, feels good-initially, is fun, helps me forget problems.	Expensive, bad judgment, makes me angry, fighter, irresponsible, lazy, or endangers lives.
Gossip	Minimizes my problems, puts focus on others, and makes me look or feel better.	Denial, hurts others, guilt, anger, dishonest, or two faced.
Pornography	Gives a sense of worthiness, a fantasy, an imaginative journey where I'm in full control, A feeling of being desired and wanted.	Guilt, feeling unworthy, remorseful, dirty, degrading, out of control, or unrealistic expectations.

Summary

Points to ponder-

We can't avoid pain, only manage it.

Pain separates winners and losers.

In the long run, losing is more painful than winning.

What would a winner do?

Face pain and if it's purposeful, welcome it.

Use bad pain as a motivator to focus on solutions.

Chapter 15
Fear

Winners take chances. Like everyone else, they fear failing, but they refuse to let fear control them. – Unknown

Since it's natural to avoid pain, we are faced with challenges even when there is a purpose. Here are a few obstacles that will detour our focus from our desires.

Confidence	**Faith/Belief**
Lack of interest	**Value**
Motivation	**Cost**
Hard work	**Time**
Procrastination	**Knowledge**
Forgetfulness	**Disorganization**

There are other obstacles but when pain is involved, you can count on the underlying cancer known as fear. Before saying too much more about fear, I want to set the stage.

I hope it's obvious to you that I try my best to live and think positively. I truly believe we should live, eat, and breathe the good, the clean, the pure, and the positive ways of life. I am no fan of focusing on the negative; however, I must also be realistic and acknowledge the dangers of bad fear. This is not to focus on fear but to identify, learn from, and expose it in detail. Fear is a very powerful thing that can and does keep many people from being the winner they were born to be.

The Fear of Fear

We have the power to beat fear, provided, we understand and fear the fear itself. There is good fear, the kind of fear for a supreme power, as in reverence, respect, or awe. I have a huge amount of good fear for my God. I have good fear for my mother. When he was alive, I had good fear for my step-father. I had good fear for my drill sergeant in the Army. These are very healthy and needed fears. Many of us have a healthy fear for traffic, hurricanes, fire, and poison. We respect and understand their power. Life would be more challenging if we touched a hot burner every time we used a stove. Fortunately, most of us learned to fear hot burners as a child and now we get to use them for our benefit. This is the kind of good fear (respect) you and I need for the bad fear.

Bad fear, on the other hand, multiplies the potential negative outcomes. It enhances our perception of pain and will very easily create a false picture. You have probably walked on a neighborhood sidewalk many times with a high percentage of success. Put the same exact sidewalk on the side of a mountain, five hundred feet off the ground, without guard rails, and it's a different story. An NFL field goal kicker will make the kick thousands of times during practice and regular season games. Put him in that same situation at the end of the Super Bowl with his final kick as the deciding win or loss for the team and everything changes. Why? There is now a *great* fear of loss, of embarrassment, of being less valuable, of not being accepted, of losing some love. Fear changes the picture dramatically. It's common for the other team to call a *timeout* to purposely drag out the moment. This allows the fear to grow even more. Confidence decreases while stress and anxiety increases. Everything else being equal, the kicker's inner security will ultimately determine if the fear is large enough to negatively affect him.

What are some of your fears? Is it heights, public speaking, insects, loneliness, or the unknown? Is it possible that our obstacles in life are rooted by the fear of pain? What could ever be worse than pain? The only thing I can possibly think of is - unfamiliar pain, which is still a fear of pain. If love is our ultimate desire and pain is our biggest fear, is it possible that our ultimate fear is pain from the lack of love? We

Chapter 15: Fear

can overcome these fears by recognizing good pain and gaining from it. The more we fill ourselves with love, the less fear we carry.

Empire State Building

In December 2004, I took my daughter, who was ten, to New York for Christmas. As expected, we had a blast. While there, we decided to go to the top of the Empire State Building. I am not a huge fan of heights. As we were going up the elevator, fear was trying to slowly creep in my mind, but only creeping. Being the positive-thinking, energetic fela' I am, I wasn't about to allow fear to whoop up on me!

Prior to reaching the top, around the eightieth floor, the elevator stopped. We had to get out and walk through an observatory room. The room had a roped-off walkway and open windows, which allows people to enjoy a spectacular view - so I have been told. My daughter and our friends enjoyed the view. I stayed as far away from the windows as possible. I made absolutely sure that I looked inward at the walls as I successfully navigated my way through the ropes and out of the room. At that point, fear was no longer just creeping inside of me. It was flowing faster than high-speed internet. But I was still trying to stay positive. Then we had to get back in the elevator and continue to the top. Only twenty more floors!

The elevator had the typical crack in the floor that you walk over when you get in or out - the tiny opening between the elevator and the building. It must have been the fear in me that prompted me to be concerned. Perhaps it was subconsciously, but I felt the need to look through that tiny opening as I stepped across and into the elevator. I am not sure if I will be able to fairly describe to you the picture I saw as I looked through that crack. The crack itself immediately became about three feet wide. Well, it did in my mind! And I saw nothing but air, way down there, it went on forever. The elevator closed and fear was wearing me out! Worse, I was trapped in the elevator going up! I am not a math major but I do know if I saw air going way down and I was still headed up that meant more air and more fear.

My palms were moist, my eyes were big, my heart was racing, and my daughter was laughing. At ten years old, she was afraid of...nothing. I literally became nauseous and had all kinds of fearful thoughts. *The elevator could break. The Empire State Building could* come down. *What if this happens or what if that happens?* I literally imprisoned myself with my silly (very serious at that moment) thoughts. I stayed in the elevator when it reached the top floor. "I'll meet you at the bottom," I said, with a weak voice, to my daughter and friends. The ride down was one of the longest of my life. I experienced even more sweaty palms, cotton mouth, and piercing thoughts full of the burning acid called fear. I finally made my way to the bottom and gratefully waited.

Fear vs. Winning

Fear paralyzes and prohibits us from so many things in life. My example is one of millions and is easy to spot because it's obvious. Unfortunately, fear is not always easy to spot and will often camouflage many of our insecurities. Fear can be like a huge rock we bury under the ground. We can cover it up, try to avoid it, and ignore it, but it still weighs the same under the surface. It will still hold us down. This deadly fear we are discussing does not mix with winning. It does not come from love. In the Bible we are told God does not give us the spirit of fear, but of power, love, and sound mind[16]. There is no fear in perfect love. Therefore, negative fear drives you away from winning. When we are confronted with pain, we will face it if we have enough inner love or faith to handle the situation. However, if fear dominates over our level of faith or love, we will avoid it or run. This is called fight or flight syndrome.

Fear Distorts Our Focus

We promise according to our hopes and perform according to our fears - François de la Rochefoucauld

Fear will make us change our focus, sometimes without even realizing it. I will use an analogy of driving, on what I call, the winner's highway. Fear becomes the tollbooth between us and our desires. It fools us into thinking the toll is too high and the pain has no purpose. Or that the pain is too unbearable.

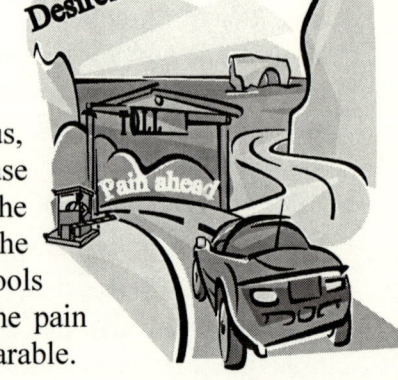

Chapter 15: Fear

When this picture is painted in the mind, our desires become less visible and we start looking for exit ramps off the winner's highway. As mentioned earlier, those roads (detours) have fear and pain on them also, usually bad pain.

Have you ever been on a dead-end road in life? I have been on several of them. Thank God we are able to make U-turns. Are you tired of running in circles with a particular issue? Would you like to refocus your efforts? You are capable of redirecting your life and re-entering the winner's highway.

It's not the pain that changes our focus and steers us the wrong way. Rather, it's the fear of the pain. Once we learn how to stay focused on our purpose, we are able to overcome the fear, pay the toll, drive on, and face the pain. The people who stay on the winner's highway the most are those who know how to get through the tolls of fear.

Align Focus with Desires

We get what we focus on in life, not necessarily what we desire. Desires may be valid but constant focus is revealed in the end. A lot of our desires are on the other side of the toll booths, through the gates of pain. However, the fear of that pain can distort our focus and keep us away from those dreadful tolls and, seemingly, out of harms way. When this happens, we switch our focus to what we *think* is a safe detour.

Fear gives us the false perception or the illusion that the temporary satisfaction of the detour is much easier and comforting to focus on than our current desire. It lures us into thinking it's sunny and better. Our current desires require much more effort. They require facing pain in which fear has magnified and distorted. Sometimes fear will make little or no pain look like a lot of pain. Looking through the window of fear makes a minnow look like a shark. Then irrational thoughts occur like, "Why would I want to go through the pain of becoming smoke-free when it is so much easier to keep smoking?" This may sound ridiculous, but we think like this daily, to one degree or the other. Drug addicts may want to be free of drugs, but the fear of going through detoxification and all the other pains associated with getting clean may distort their focus. Focusing on the next fix is less painful, initially. So they take the detour once again. They end up staying high rather than free. Alcoholics may want to stay sober but focusing on the drink keeps them intoxicated. Food addicts may want to lose weight or become healthier but focusing on the food keeps them overeating. <u>Once we get our focus in line with our desires, we then have a match that works.</u> Many people *desire* to change but continue to *focus* on and receive the opposite.

Fear tolls are all over the winner's highway. They're often camouflaged in forms such as anger, pain, resentment, bitterness, and self-pity. Zig Ziglar says fear forms an acrostic for *false evidence appearing real*. My friend Mike Polachek leads a group at our church called Celebrate Recovery. It's an outreach ministry for people with hurts, habits, or hang-ups. He says fear stands for *future events appearing real*. The more you and I fill our inner fuel tank with love, the easier we can drive through the fear tolls and stay on the winner's highway of life.

To a degree, because of fear, all of us have hurts, habits, or hang-ups. Fear says "*Why go through counseling with a mate, learn to forgive, rekindle positive emotions, or hang in there?* Divorce seems like the satisfying answer. *Why take off of work early, lose the overtime pay, or miss the promotion?* The kids can entertain themselves on a video game at home alone. *Why allow myself to believe in an unseen God, read the Bible, pray, or risk being labeled as weak?* I can simply attempt to stay in full control. *Why work hard, be responsible, treat people kindly, or be a giver?* It seems much easier to be a taker."

Chapter 15: Fear

Of course you already know many of these options usually end up being very painful without a purpose.

Like the illustration a few pages ago, when we take a detour, fear can convince us that the detour is actually the appropriate path. Our egos are quite good at weaving in beliefs to fit our current motives or agenda. Fear will help us bury our true desires and leave them back on the "old path," the one where the tolls and pain exist. It will convince us to settle; to believe our current focus is our desire (or new desire). Instead of dealing with the pain, it is easier to change our *desires* to match our current or new focus.

We may know that the road we are currently heading down (focus) is the wrong way because it was a detour. But, sometimes we are afraid of going down the road we really want (true desires). Here is another way to see this view point. When we wish to change, one of two things happens.

- We change our focus to match our desires. This results in **changed** behavior.

- We change our desires to match our current focus. This results in **unchanged** behavior.

Suppose I weighed 250 pounds and desired to weigh 180 pounds. I must change my focus toward the 180 pounds in order to reach that desire. It would take initial pain such as discipline, commitment, inconvenience, exercise, and giving up certain foods. I must have enough love inside of me to fuel the necessary amount of faith and hope it takes to change my focus in order to face the pain. If not, fear will discourage me every time. Then I will use excuses in order to justify my current focus and make my current situation, (250 pounds) acceptable and okay. Amazingly, this whole process can happen consciously and subconsciously within seconds. Henry C. Link said "While one person hesitates because he feels inferior, the other is busy making mistakes and becoming superior."

This leads to, what psychologists call - denial. We make our problem (the current focus we wish to change) okay and acceptable. We are then able to claim we do not have the problem anymore. After all, if we make the 250 pounds okay in our mind, then it is no longer considered a problem. Open up most hurts or wounds and fear will be in there somewhere. You can practically trace any negative behavior or emotion back to fear.

Just ask yourself, "how is fear linked to my _____(insert any negative behavior or emotion). What am I afraid of or what am I running from?" It could be a challenge with forgiveness, depression, stress, staying healthy, relationships, lack of money, or many others. It may not even seem to make sense on the surface, but fear is buried in there somewhere. The quicker we expose it, the quicker we can face it. Fear can drive us to unknowingly do all kinds of things to fill insecurities. The very fact that it makes us insecure will blindly motivate us to do things we don't want to do and know we shouldn't do. Fear has a way of convincing us that life will not be as good, cool, or calm without certain things. Fear will be around as long as you are and it's always willing to get in the way of you and your desires - if you allow it. Fear multiplies and spreads like a fungus, and we should avoid it like the plague.

Summary

Points to ponder-

Have you identified the fears that hold you back?

Hidden or subconscious fear can hold us back.

Fear will motivate us to detour from the winner's highway.

Love drives out fear.

What would a winner do?

Focus on the gain, not the fear of the pain.

Respect fear and learn from it.

Part V: I Gauge My Growing, Giving, and Gaining

Chapter 16
Goals

Give me a stockclerk with a goal, and I'll give you a man who will make history. Give me a man with no goals, and I'll give you a stockclerk. – James Cash (JC) Penny

Until an action becomes a habit, it helps to have a system that keeps us going in the proper direction. A goals system clearly defined and kept in focus will assist us in becoming a master executioner. We spend 24 hours of every day *doing* something. Whether it is sleeping, working, singing, eating, or *doing* any number of other things. Without becoming any smarter or working any harder, we can apply minor adjustments in order to enjoy life more today, while avoiding a lot of pain later. The reality is, you will live by a system either managed by life or managed by you. Manage your past and present or it will manage you. Life is not only a "to do" list, life is also a "did" list. The management of those lists will say a lot about how often we win.

Do I Have a Deal for You

I suppose you have been car shopping before and used the negotiation process in order to get the best price possible. What if the following hypothetical scenario happens the next time you are negotiating?

You are really desperate for a vehicle. You have spent way too much money on your current one. You really need the best deal possible. You are looking at a new car and the salesperson suddenly remembers a special deal; a huge discount on a factory blemished car similar to the one you are currently looking at. You get excited. The clerk out back is called and asked to drive the car around front so you can see it. As you wait, the salesperson proceeds to describe this magnificent deal. It just happens to be exactly what you want - color, bells, whistles, and all. The salesperson offers it to you for half price! Here is the opportunity to realistically save thousands. What a steal! As the salesperson continues describing the car, the clerk pulls around and it catches your eye. Sure enough, you have found the steal of the century. It is beautiful! You are excited. You're happier than a baby with a new poodle. Caught up in the excitement, you forgot all about the factory blemish. As you get closer to the car, you notice the windshield is different. You are told the car was accidentally made with a solid black windshield and the factory has determined it is impossible to modify. The salesperson explains that this is why it comes with such a deep discount. And then goes on to remind you it is a small price to pay for *all* the savings. You are insulted, upset, and frustrated! You cannot believe the nerve of this person. You feel as let down as the cruise director for the Titanic! With all the patience you have left, you kindly say to the salesperson, "I cannot believe you expect me to endanger myself and others. This is ridiculous and the vehicle should be outlawed. How in the world could I ever get to my destination if I could not see where I am going?" Then you leave the dealership.

Your question would be a great one and worth repeating. *How in the world could you ever get to your destination if you could not see it?* I have a better question for you. How could you ever get to a destination that you don't even have? Everyday, many people jump in a car with a black windshield and head down the highway of life.

On the contrary, there is nothing wrong with a relaxing Sunday drive to nowhere, they are wonderful. You get to drive around and sightsee with no sense of urgency. You don't have to be concerned with road signs of any kind, no mile markers, road names, or city names. Those tools are only useful if you need to know where you are headed. Life is full of tools to help you get where you want to go, provided you know where that is. The problem is, we have too many Sunday drivers Monday through Saturday.

Testing Your Aim

At a major university, a professor of economics gave a test to his class. He handed out three separate pages with a different series of test questions on each page. The students were to pick only one page of questions for their test. The first page of questions was the hardest and was worth 50 points. The second page was not quite as hard and worth 40 points. The third, the easiest, was worth only 30 points. When the students had taken the test and turned in the papers, the students who had chosen the hardest questions, or the 50-point questions, were given A's. The students who had chosen the 40-point questions were given B's, and those who chose the 30-point questions, or the easiest questions, were given C's. Whether or not their answers were correct was not considered. Understandably, the students were confused and asked the professor how he had graded the exam. The professor simply explained, "I was not testing your knowledge, I was testing your aim."

Roadmap for the Winner's Highway

The last part of the wishlist (T), the **t**arget, will be very difficult to reach if you do not have one. Once we have a target, we must then have a proper method or *plan* to get there. The winner's highway requires a roadmap. Most of us would not take off on a long journey across the nation without a map. It makes no sense to go through the journey of life without one either. I am talking about goal setting and having a goals system.

Everybody has goals. You have a goal, I hope, to get something out of this book. Students have goals to pass tests. Parents have goals to raise good children. Companies have goals to be profitable. But a goals system, now that is a whole different story. A goals *system* is the roadmap for the winner's highway.

The Day Before Vacation

I learned a lot of the material I'm about to share with you from Zig Ziglar. I will ask you the same thing he has asked me, along with millions of other people. Do you agree that you get two to three times more accomplished on the day before you go on vacation than any other day of the week? Most people answer *yes* to that question. It's an amazing phenomenon that we must explore a little deeper. Rarely does a person work any harder or longer on the day before vacation, yet they accomplish so much more. Will you think back to your last day-before-vacation day? On that day, you probably felt more energetic, more confident, more purposeful, and more valuable. Wasn't your walk a little taller? Didn't you have a little more pep in your step, a little more *up* in your *giddy?* Didn't you feel better about yourself? Have you ever left for vacation earlier than planned because you accomplished everything quicker than expected?

If it's true that we get so much done and feel so good about it, why not prepare to go on vacation everyday? Why are you able to make such a huge difference in your activity, emotions, energy, and self-worth on that particular day? Could it be that you made a little effort up front that would help you reap huge benefits later? If you are like most, you sat down prior to starting that day and made a list of everything you needed to get done before going on vacation. In its simplest form, *making a list* is goal setting. You had targets and a system to help you reach those targets. You likely even did some tracking and gauging that day as well. You were also mentally prepared. Let's look at the following:

- What is a goals system
- Why have a goals system

What is a Goals System

A goals system is a written strategy intended to achieve a desired result. It is a defined and often refined process. It is gauged, measured, tracked, studied, focused upon, and adjusted. A goals system assists you in bringing your focus through a process and aligning it with your desires.

Why Have a Goals System

A goals system gives us the confidence, faith, energy, and purpose needed to overcome the fear that gets between our current focus and our unrealized desires. Failure to hit the target is never the fault of the target. A goals system will motivate you the way you were on the day before vacation. It will increase your self-image and allow you to be all you are capable of being – more of a winner. A goals system will assist you in growing to give and, interestingly enough, it will actually give you more free time.

Chapter 16: Goals

I don't know about you, but if I want something done and need another's help, I will choose a busy person over the non-busy person any day. Ironically, the busy person gets things done. They have purpose, confidence, systems, and targets. The person with little to do rarely gets much accomplished. According to Ziglar, goal setters average making 118% more than non goal setters. Additionally, surveys have proven that goal setting will help you be healthier, less stressed, happier, and more enthusiastic about life. You will enjoy more of the wishlist and, most importantly, you stay on the winner's highway more often. Amazingly, once it's in place, goal setters only spend an average of just twelve hours per month on their system. Could you imagine if we opened a business today and ran the following ad in the paper?

Could you give us twelve hours per month of your time? You must have the equivalence of a seventh grade education in math, reading, and writing skills. An imagination and willingness to plan ahead are helpful. If you have these basic traits, you are qualified and hired. In return we will increase your current income by 118%. We will decrease your heart rate and stress level. Studies show you will be happier, more enthusiastic, and enjoy more of life's wishlist. You will instantly become more of a winner in life. Please show up tomorrow morning.

Do you think we would have anyone show up? Would they be able to arrange their schedules to fit in the extra 12 hours per month? Chances are magnificent that we would have quite the long line of applicants. Do you know anyone who would apply? Would you? I would and I have. Well, today, if you desire, we will open that business, and I am going to teach you that specific system.

Summary

Points to ponder-

Would you ever settle for a black windshield on your car?

A goals system helps us see where we're going.

Missing the target is never the fault of the target.

A goals system keeps a drifter on course.

What would a winner do?

Use a goals system to move desires from dreams to reality.

Chapter 17
The Goals Process

Obstacles are those frightful things you see when you take your eyes off your goals. - Henry Ford, founder of Ford Motor Company

Balance

Just as we balance our checkbook, it's important to balance the rest of our life. Balancing simply helps us see where we have too much and where we need more. The chart below is very basic and simple. It is a great tool for helping you visually balance your wishlist instead of your wishlist balancing you. Simply circle the number you believe best describes your level for each particular area. Then connect the dots. If the connected line is not level, you are out of balance. If it is completely level, I want your autograph. I have yet to meet a person who was perfectly balanced. So don't be too concerned if your line is so bumpy it looks like a mountain climber's nightmare. The purpose here is not perfection but to give you a clearer picture.

W Wellness	I Information	S Serenity	H Hope	L Lasting Relationships	I Income	S Security	T Targets
9	9	9	9	9	9	9	9
8	8	8	8	8	8	8	8
7	7	7	7	7	7	7	7
6	6	6	6	6	6	6	6
5	5	5	5	5	5	5	5
4	4	4	4	4	4	4	4
3	3	3	3	3	3	3	3
2	2	2	2	2	2	2	2
1	1	1	1	1	1	1	1

Now you are ready to start working on your goals system. Each specific step will not apply to every goal you ever choose to set. Use what works for you. It is a learning curve, so take your time, be patient, and enjoy the rewards.

Step 1. Make a List

Make a list of everything you desire. Think big, small, long-term, short-term, tomorrow, next week, and next year. You can dream about trips, homes, careers, and friends. Use the wishlist as your guide.

Wellness – a healthy mind, body, and soul

Information – education, wisdom, and knowledge

Serenity – peace of mind

Hope – for life and the future

Lasting relationships – with substance and meaning

Income – comfortably pay bills, savings

Security – stability and safety

Targets – somewhere to aim, a direction, a purpose

The only limitation is your imagination. I highly recommend you do this list before you go to step two. It can be done in a short time once you get started. You can always add to the list later, but it's crucial for you to go ahead now - make a list. People who won't take step one never take step two. You don't have to be great to start, but you've got to start in order to be great. I will walk you through the process step by step as soon as we have some targets to work toward.

The very fact you have read this much of the book proves you want more out of life. I ask you to put it to paper and work on your list now. Include your family and get their ideas and dreams. You are more than qualified and deserve to have *written* targets. As you journey through life and have thoughts, ideas, dreams, aspirations, and desires you will want to add them to the wishlist. It's your list to view daily, weekly, or at any other desired pace. If you had all the money and time you wanted, what would be on your wishlist?

Chapter 17: The Goals Process

Wishlist						
Step 1. Wishlist	Why do I want this goal?	My goal	Final goal	Moral Fair	Grow Give	See it
Weigh 160	*To be healthier and feel better*	y	y	y	y	y

Wellness – a healthy mind, body, and soul	Step 2. Identify Final goal. Circle, underline, etc.
Information – education, wisdom, and knowledge	Step 3. Qualify "yes" to all of the questions below
Serenity – peace of mind	Did I answer, in one sentence, *why* I want this?
Hope – for life and the future	Is it *my goal* to control - not parents, spouse, etc?
Lasting relationships – with substance and meaning	Will this take me closer to my *final goal*?
Income – comfortably pay bills, savings	Is this *moral* and *fair* to all involved?
Security – stability and safety	Will this goal help me *grow* or *give*?

Step 2. Identify Final Goal

Now that you've put some targets on paper, we can go to the next step. It helps for you to identify your final destination, the very last target you desire to reach - your final goal in life. This is subject to change, but one should be identified. It would be a little tough to read a map without knowing your final destination. One of the habits in Dr Stephen Covey's book *The Seven Habits of Highly Effective People* is, Start With the End in Mind. We must know where we want to end up or we become a drifter. If you let someone else row your boat they will take it where *they* want to go.

Think about the end for a moment. Where do you see yourself? Maybe you can't see that far ahead at this moment. Try to identify the furthest point you can see. Just as you head out into the fog, go as far as you can see and then you'll be able to see further. Having an idea of the end is the foundation to your goals system. It will also assist you in thinking of more goals to add to your list. At this point, circle the one goal on your list that you see as your final goal. Remember, you can change it. A wonderful thing about a goals system is the fact it makes you think.

Step 3. Qualification

Now that you've identified a final goal you can start the qualification process. Why would anyone want to qualify a goal?

- Salespeople qualify prospects
- Detectives qualify leads
- Colleges qualify students
- Lenders qualify borrowers
- Employers qualify employees

Qualification helps to level the playing field. An unqualified goal that makes its way into your goals system is like placing the wrong road signs along a highway or in a map. It simply confuses, distracts, or voids the process.

I remember, as a child, playing around the neighborhood with my friends. At times, a lost driver would ask us for directions to their destination. Sometimes we would purposely give them the wrong directions because we thought it was cute to misinform people. While it was funny to us, the victim would unknowingly head towards a destination that was completely opposite their goal. When you and I do not qualify our goals and desires, we often, by choice, become a self-imposed victim, traveling through life toward the wrong destinations. I've been down many "rabbit trails" in life. It's quite frustrating when you determine you've gone the wrong way. By qualifying your goals, you will eliminate a lot of targets that end up as dead ends or U-turns. Keeping the *qualified* targets in sight will ensure a safer, less stressful, more effective, and productive journey. Since your final goal will be the anchor to your goals system, I recommend you qualify it first. This can be done by asking yourself the following questions.

Wishlist						
Step 1. Wishlist	Why do I want this goal?	My goal	Final goal	Moral Fair	Grow Give	See it
Weigh 160	To be healthier and feel better	y	y	y	y	y

Qualification Questions

- **Can I answer, in one sentence, why I want this goal?**

If you can not answer in one sentence *why* this is your goal then it isn't clear enough at this point.

- **Is it <u>my</u> goal to control, not my parents, spouse, etc?**

This goal has to be yours; you cannot become a doctor for your parents or children. The goal must also be yours to control. I want the Tampa Bay Bucs football team to win the Super Bowl every year, but so far they've only listened to me once. In other words, I have no control over the outcome. Therefore, it is not *my* goal. This is very important because it's easy to get occupied trying to do things we have no control over.

- **Will this take me closer to my final goal?**

If this goal will not take you closer to your final goal, then it *will* take you further away.

- **Is this moral and fair to all involved?**

This is a great chance to think about your children, spouse, parents, friends, etc.

- **Will this goal help me grow or give?**

As we've already discussed, growing and giving are the foundations of winning. If your goals are not helping you win, then they're helping you_____?

- **Do I see myself reaching this goal?**

Until you see it, chances are you won't pursue it. The body follows the eyes whether those eyes are between your ears, a Seeing Eye dog, or other means.

If you can't answer "yes" to *all* of the questions, then at this time you do not have a qualified goal - simply a dream or a wish. There's nothing wrong with dreams and wishes; this is where it all starts. However, they should stay on the wishlist and not be moved into the goals system until they meet *all* of the qualifications.

Once you have a *qualified* goal to focus on, it should come off of your wishlist. The wishlist should constantly change by adding new items and removing or promoting others. The idea is to process the goal through the qualification stage, remove it, and add it to a Goals Achievement Process (GAP) sheet. This is the process that fills the "gap" between desires and results (wants vs. action).

Goals Achievement Process (GAP)

The big secret in life is that there is no big secret. Whatever your goal, you can get there if you're willing to work.
 - Oprah Winfrey, American TV Personality

Steps 4-10 of the goals process are completed on a goals achievement process (GAP) sheet. The GAP sheet is just like a work order, invoice, or job order - the details are shown up top and the actual line items are listed on the bottom.

Write the name of your goal in the upper right-hand corner. Try to turn passive goals into proactive goals. A goal to lose weight, get rid of a smoking habit, or stop being lazy are all negative tense (losing something) and become difficult targets.

It's tough to work hard to *lose* something. You can not properly focus on something if it's not there. Instead, try to re-word the goal to a positive tense, make it a *gain*. A goal to reach a certain weight, become smoke free, or work harder will paint a picture in your mind of a target you desire. It's tough to "see" a loss of something because it's, well, lost or gone.

Chapter 17: The Goals Process

Goals Achievement Process (GAP)		Goal	160 pounds	
Step 4. Benefits	Live longer	Feel better		Track
Look better	More energy	Higher self-image		%
				100
Step 5. Specify	Size na	Actual 200 pounds		90
Color na	Style na	Difference (**Action Focus**)		80
Model/Yr na	Weight na	Burn, trim, bury 40 pounds		70
Step 6. Small steps (where applicable, break goal down into bite-size measurements)				60
Start Date 01.01.08	Achievement Date 04.01.08	Length 4 days/wk/mth		50
Per min na	Per day 5.6 oz	Per month 10 pounds		40
Per hour na	Per week 2.5 pounds	Per year na		30
Step 7. Possible obstacles				
Need more nutritional education, love sweets, enjoy eating late at night				
Step 8. Action list (people involved, tools needed, things to buy, etc.)			S = Sub goal	
Order	Action, Task list	S	✓ Cost	Time
2	Walk 3 times per week			3 hrs
3	Eat up to 2000 calories per day (this item has a new Gap sheet)	s		
1	Drink 8 – 10 glasses of water per day			
Step 9. Commitment (consider total cost, time, and balance)		Total		3 hrs
Balance – W I S H L I S T (circle or underline no more than two)				
Commitment date 01.01.08				
Step 10. Notes/Tracking				
I can do this. Anyone can burn 5.6 oz per day! Pay attention to page 2 for calories and types of foods. I was born to win!				

Step 4. Benefits

Write down all of the benefits you will gain from this goal. This will fuel your actions the most. The more benefits you list, the more motives or reasons you have for reaching your goal.

Step 5. Specify

Some of this will apply to your specific goal; some won't, depending on the goal. The more specific you are, the clearer it will be. Try a white, four-door, automatic car; or a two-story home, with swimming pool, on one acre. Not just a home or a car. If at all possible to measure, you want to fill in the two boxes labeled *actual* and *difference*. The box labeled *actual* is where you will put your current position in relation to the goal you want. The *actual* box will have a value that's measurable - money, pounds, time, or other measure. After knowing the *goal* vs. the *actual* you can then determine the *difference*. Knowing the difference is very important. This is your focus point. In many cases you do not need to focus on reaching your full goal because you have already reached some of it. If you want a four year degree and already have one and a half years of college, you only need to focus on two and a half more years, not the full four-year degree. This is why knowing the *difference* is so powerful. If you have a goal to save $100 and you've already saved $60, it's much easier to focus on saving $40(difference) rather than $100. Here are some examples of different measures and focus points.

Goal	Actual	Difference
Where you want to go	Where you are now	Difference between each
160 lbs	200lbs	40lbs
Car($30k)	Car(15k)	$15K
Home($300k)	Home($150K)	$150k
4 yr degree	1.5yrs	2.5yrs

Specifying may take a little extra effort in the beginning, but reaching your goals becomes much more obtainable. It also helps you identify traction and momentum. The space shuttle uses more fuel to take off than it uses on the rest of the trip[17]. Knowing you have already "taken off" is a huge part of reaching your goals.

Step 6. Small Steps

Continue to work your goal down to a manageable size in money, time, weight, or other. It's so much easier to burn five pounds per month than thirty pounds in the next half year. Five pounds per month is only a little over a pound per week. Breaking it down into small chunks makes reaching your goal more of a reality.

Step 7. Possible Obstacles

This step has personally been one of my largest challenges in life - not considering possible obstacles down the road. You may know exactly what I'm talking about. Wars are lost because they are launched before considering possible obstacles. This is not an area to focus on but it is important to review. Imagine if commercial planes flew all over the world without aviators ever checking the weather. Some would make the trip okay, but the odds are in our favor when they know the possibility of certain obstacles.

Goals Achievement Process (GAP)		Goal 160 pounds	
Step 4. Benefits	*Live longer*	*Feel better*	Track
Look better	*More energy*	*Higher self image*	%
			100
Step 5. Specify	Size *na*	Actual 200 pounds	90
Color *na*	Style *na*	Difference (**Action Focus**)	80
Model/Yr *na*	Weight *na*	*Burn, trim, bury 40 pounds*	70
Step 6. Small steps (where applicable, break goal down into bite-size measurements)			60
Start Date 01.01.08	Achievement Date 04.01.08	Length 4 days/wk/mth	50
Per min *na*	Per day 5.6 *oz*	Per month 10 *pounds*	40
Per hour *na*	Per week 2.5 *pounds*	Per year *na*	30
Step 7. Possible obstacles			
Nutritional education, love sweets, enjoy eating late at night			

Step 8. Action list (people involved, tools needed, things to buy, etc.)				S = Sub goal		
Order	Action, Task list				S	✓	Cost	Time
2	*Walk 3 times per week*						3 *hrs*
3	*Eat up to 2000 calories per day (this item has a new Gap sheet)*					✓	
1	*Drink 8 - 10 glasses of water per day*						

Step 8. Action List

This will be your actual task list or "to do" list to reach your goal.

Order – after you have made your list, you can prioritize the order of which one to do first, second, etc.

Action - the actual task that you will do. This is where you list all of your separate tasks for completing your goal.

S - Check here if this is a sub-goal of the goal. If it is a sub-goal you need to create a new sheet (*Goal Achievement Process*) and work this sub-goal just as you worked the main goal. Here's an example.

Assume you had a goal of *a new home*. There would be many different task items associated with that goal. Several of those tasks would need their own goal sheet because they would have their own tasks, specific to them. Things like "decorate home, install a pool, and landscaping." All of these are tasks for the main goal, but they are actually goals themselves. Imagine trying to do everything involved with installing a pool without having a separate worksheet for it. I want to make this as clear as possible. A task for one goal can also be a goal itself, in another relationship, with other tasks.

Goal – New home
- Task – Decorate
- Task – Build Pool
- Task – Landscape

In the *relation* above, **build pool** is a task of the goal - **new home**.

Goal – New home
- Task – Decorate
- Task – Build Pool
  - **Build Pool**(create new GAP worksheet as a new **goal**)
    - Clear trees
    - Dig hole
    - Poor concrete
    - Fill with water
- Task – Landscape

Although building a pool is still a task for the new home, it's also a separate goal. Just as a man is a son in relation to his father, but the same man can also be a father to his own son. It all depends on the relationship. He is the same person with two different titles. Just like a topic in one area of life could, itself, be a sub-topic in another.

Why is this important to know? Here's what can happen if goals/sub-goals are not dealt with properly. You can be working a goal through the process and everything's going great. You're excited, you have momentum, and then **it** happens. The *system* does not have a spot for a particular detail. Or it does not have room for an extra step or task. Pretty soon, you end up trying to complete the goal without working the process – which defeats a goals *system*. If you have ever worked a goals system you may know what I am talking about. If a particular task requires its own unique set of micro-managed steps, it is important that you make a new worksheet. Otherwise, you're back to doing it without a goals system.

✓ - Check this box when you've completed the individual task. Some of these individual task items will be repeated over and over. I personally circle the ones which I know I will repeat. Drinking eight glasses of water per day as part of a healthy goal would be an example of a repeated task. This is your goal; work it the way that fits for you - circle, highlight, underline, etc.

Cost – cost or expense of the task, if applicable

Time – how long the task will take, if applicable

Step 9. Commitment (consider total cost, time, and balance)	Total	3 hrs
Balance – W I S H L I S T (circle or underline no more than two)		
Commitment date 01.01.08		
Step 10. Notes/Tracking		
I can do this. Anyone can burn 5.6 oz per day! Pay attention to page 2 for calories and types of foods. I was born to win!		

Step 9. Commitment

If you cannot or will not work your goal, don't commit yet. Consider the total cost, time, and obstacles. Pray about it. Look at your balance chart on your wishlist. Circle no more than two areas from your balance chart where this goal applies. In some cases it could apply to more than two areas but circle the two it applies to the most. If this is an income goal and your chart clearly shows that you're already way up on the *income* area, you may want to reconsider whether you have other goals that need to be worked on first.

Step 10. Notes/tracking

This is a good area to write any reminders or encouraging words. Things that will help you work more toward your goal. If I could encourage you to write anything, it would be a personal message to yourself - *I was born to win!*

Summary

Points to ponder-

Until you have an idea of your final goal in life, how do you know if your other goals really matter?

A goals system takes time and effort initially, but the investment will give you more of a return than a stock or bank account.

What would a winner do?

Work my goals system.

Chapter 18
A System for Action

When you engage in systematic, purposeful action, using and stretching your abilities to the maximum, you cannot help but feel positive and confident about yourself. - Brian Tracy, Trainer, Speaker

Fast Food Systems

When I was a teenager, I worked at a few different fast food restaurants. All of them had one thing in common - you must learn the system first. The goal was basic; give the customer a good value in trade for the customer's money. The system was simple. Take the order, prepare and/or package the food, and deliver it to the customer. I think it is fascinating that a group, made up primarily of teenagers, is able to consistently and effectively get so much accomplished. Often times they are under tremendous pressures of multitasking, time deadlines, and customers who are demanding. Simple systems help ensure they are more effective. A system helps us focus on what we're going *to* (targets), not what we're going *through*.

What He Stands For

Through Zig Ziglar's company, I had the privilege of meeting a very special man named John Foppe. He speaks at Ziglar's "Born to Win" seminars in Dallas. John is one of the most inspiring people I have ever met. John's humble spirit is apparent from the beginning. He's very genuine and exposes little facts that you and I might hide. Unusual things, like his clip-on neck tie that uses Velcro instead of a clip. It wasn't long before he was taking off his shoes and socks, on stage! Being raised in a southern town, I didn't think that was too unusual. He even throws his feet on the table right there in front of you. Then, the way he drinks from a cup and proceeds to tell his story is amazing. The ways he shook my hand and signed his book afterward were equally impressive.

Considering John Foppe was born without arms seem to keep him genuine and humble. You see, John uses his feet for the same things you and I use our hands. He's a great artist who likes to draw and paint. He drives with his feet, using a regular vehicle with no special equipment. He can cook, do the dishes, dress himself, and type at 63 wpm! As I am writing this, he and his wife just had their first baby.

Prior to being married, he traveled around the country by himself, speaking and encouraging people. He has a master's degree in clinical social work. He has written a book called "Armed with Hope." And he owns a seminar and consulting company. John says he has to be more creative in a day than most of us have to be in a month. I could spend a lot of time telling you a lot of things about this winner. I have learned to appreciate him and what he stands for, both literally and figuratively speaking.

The main point I want to make is this - John Foppe has one system after another in place that enables him to function in everyday life. He does not have a choice. The reality is, neither do you and I. John says, "We should not confuse simple with easy. The actions that make success are simple, but often the execution of those actions is not easy."

Slow Down to Speed Up

When astronauts orbit the earth, the slower they go, the faster they go. As the shuttle slows down, the earth's gravity brings it closer to our planet causing a tighter orbit and faster speed. When the shuttle speeds up, it moves away from the earth and its orbit is larger which makes the spacecraft move slower.

A master of slowing down to speed up, John Wooden, the legendary basketball coach, won 10 NCAA basketball championships at UCLA, the last in 1975. Nobody has ever come within six of him. He won 88 straight games between January 1971, and January 1974. Nobody has come within 42 since. He would spend a half hour the first day of practice teaching his men how to put on a sock. He would warn them that wrinkles could lead to blisters. Those huge players would sneak

Chapter 18: A System for Action

looks at one another and roll their eyes. Eventually, they would do it right. "Good," he'd say, "and now the other foot." He would make them slow down so they could ultimately speed up.

You have been given a lot of information on how to stay on the winner's highway. Putting the information into action is the real key. We must close the gap between knowing versus doing. It has been said that the body of water between knowledge and application is one of the largest masses of water in the world. There are many books and seminar materials sitting on shelves. They are covered with dust on the outside and a wealth of knowledge on the inside. We have the knowledge, but the application always seems to be the bigger challenge - the *doing* what we *know* to do. When it is all said and done there is usually more said than done. I am convinced we are so busy trying to get ahead that we fall behind. You must slow down long enough to manage life; if not, life will manage you.

Automatic Actions

I am your constant companion. I am your greatest helper or your heaviest burden. I will push you onward or drag you down to failure. I am completely at your command. Half the things you do, you might just as well turn over to me. I will be able to do them quickly and correctly. I am easily managed. Show me exactly how you want something done and after a few lessons I will do it automatically. I am the servant of all great men and sadly of all failures as well. Those who are great, I have made great. Those who are failures, I have made failures. I am not a machine, though I work with all the precision of a machine plus the intelligence of a human. You may run me for profit or run me for ruin; it makes no difference to me. Take me, train me, be firm with me, and I will put the world at your feet. Be easy with me, and I will destroy you. Who am I? I am a habit!

A habit, like cruise control, is a wonderful thing when used to our advantage. But sometimes cruise control can be dangerous. When I was in the Army, I bought a classic '69 Mustang. I rebuilt the motor, re-upholstered the inside, gave it a new paint job, bought new wheels, tires, and more. I practically restored it from the ground up. One thing I added, which was not an original item, was a cruise control system.

It was not too difficult to install and I must admit I enjoyed having the luxury of cruise control on such an old car.

One day my enjoyment changed. I was sitting at a traffic light waiting for it to turn green when my cruise control took on a mind of its own. Have you ever had a computerized device do such a thing? Or have you ever been abducted by a car? My car took off and ran right through the traffic signal. Thank God no other cars or people were in the way (I'm glad I didn't have to explain this to a police officer). I was certainly surprised to learn my car was accelerating and even more surprised when I wasn't able to stop it! It was kind of like being on a horse that's out of control. The only thing going faster than the car was my heartbeat. I was finally able to reach under the dash and pull a fuse to stop the cruise-*out of*-control.

Do you have things in your life that are cruising out of control? You can replace them with positive habits that will cruise you *into* control. Once a good habit is in place, like the bad ones, it's an automatic system. Automatic systems control more of you than you think - literally.

Conscious and Subconscious

We are what we repeatedly do. Excellence then is not an act, but a habit. - Aristotle

Our choices are generated from two sources: conscious and subconscious (automatic) mind.

A conscious choice, otherwise known as *thinking* or *cognition,* is basically the process of being *aware* of information that flows through our thoughts and emotions. It looks like this:

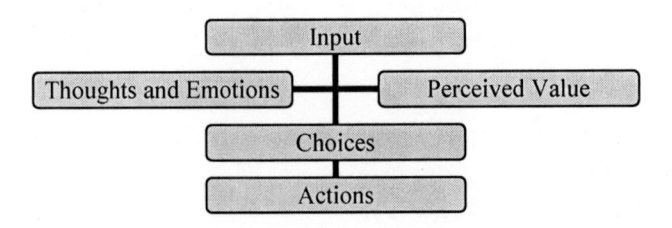

```
                    Input
Thoughts and Emotions ─┼─ Perceived Value
                   Choices
                   Actions
```

There are other variables in the process – motive, personality, environment, experiences, biology, spirituality, influence, and more.

Chapter 18: A System for Action

Our mind processes all of these different variables within milliseconds. If just one piece of the process is out of balance, emotions for example, then the outcome can be disastrous. This is why our thinking is so important and to do it properly takes constant effort, practice, skill, ability, motivation, commitment, and desire.

The subconscious mind is a whole other world that science is still learning a lot about. It's responsible for actions outside of the conscious mind, like telling our eyes to blink or grinding our teeth. It stores images, sounds, knowledge, and other information. Actions generated from our subconscious mind bypass the conscious (awareness) process. This can be very exciting!

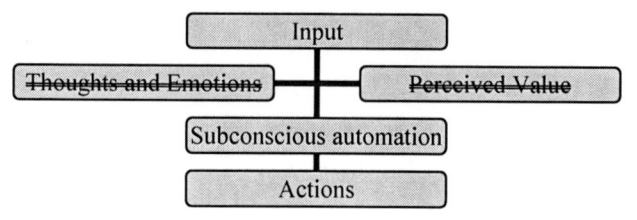

```
                    Input
                      |
    Thoughts and Emotions --+-- Perceived Value
                      |
         Subconscious automation
                      |
                   Actions
```

It's like sending a letter around the world via email rather than sticking the letter in your mailbox. Both require processes, but email is automatic and regular mail is not. The automation eliminates so many possible obstacles. It's easy to see why any of us would want to add more **positive** actions to the automation process (our subconscious). If we repeat actions enough, we do just that, and they become habits.

Habits are actually programmed into our subconscious mind. Once the input arrives, the subconscious mind automatically (habitually) delivers the action. I wear a seatbelt, do you? Each time I get in my vehicle my habit kicks in and I put on my seatbelt. I could be on the phone, cranking the car, talking, or drinking water. Regardless, my seatbelt goes on without me consciously thinking about it.

The encyclopedia refers to habits as such: *habituation is a fundamental or basic process of biological systems and does not require conscious motivation or awareness to occur.* It could be a habit such as biting fingernails, scratching, or chewing on your inner cheek. I personally have a habit of tapping someone's arm when I am speaking to them. My brother, Andy, will often point this out and remind me that I am doing it. When he brings it to my attention, it makes me laugh because I am literally unaware of this action.

Do you remember when you first learned to drive? It was a carefully thought-out process from your conscious mind. *Put both hands on the wheel. Always remember the blinker. Look in the rear view mirror. Stay the proper car length behind the car in front of you, etc.* Do you think about that stuff anymore? Now you are able to drive, talk on the phone, primp, drink coffee, roll down the window, and discipline the kids in the back seat - all at the same time! It seems natural, because it is now in your subconscious, an automatic action – a habit.

The most rewarding part of a habit, in my opinion, is the fact it bypasses the emotional part of the thinking process - anger, guilt, sadness, stress. And what about that deadly emotion I spent so much time on earlier; *fear?* Habits give none of them the time of day! With habits, negative emotions are now sharks reduced to minnows. Ferocious lions turned into kitty cats. Are you starting to like habits now? Do you have any habits? Of course you do, we are creatures of habit.

Because of your natural ability to take on habits, you can choose to implement the ones that promote the good, the clean, the pure, and the positive. Sooner or later, good habits will drown out bad ones. Good habits will happily pay those tolls of fear on the winner's highway.

Summary

Points to ponder-

"The system you're currently using is perfectly designed for the results you're getting." – Dr. W. Edward Deming

Habits are capable of bypassing emotions.

What would a winner do?

Purposely replace bad habits with good habits.

Chapter 19
Tracking and Gauging

I guess we've always known that information gives you a certain power, but the degree to which we can retrieve it in our computer really does give us the power of competitive advantage.
– Sam Walton, founder of Wal-Mart

I have many of the same daily challenges that you may have. I want to avoid anger, fear, stress, feelings of rejection, and other pain. Like you, I also desire to be patient, caring, loving, kind, positive, and responsible. Until those desires become habits we must stay *focused* (as we discussed in chapter 15) and constantly repeat them. Tracking and gauging helps us accomplish both - focus and repetition. It empowers us with information specific to our personal growth, traction, and momentum. Having this information will keep you hopeful and interested. Being interested ensures you will stay focused long enough to create a new habit.

Imagine how ineffective and troublesome it would be if we never knew how much fuel was in our vehicle. Just as we need to gauge the fuel in our cars, we should also gauge the fuel in our life.

The chart on the next page is designed to help you track things about yourself and create new habits. It is also set up so that, both consciously and subconsciously, you will learn about other people. The beauty is - all of this takes places simultaneously.

Why is it important to learn about others? As winners, our ultimate goal is to obtain love. We already know the way we do this is by giving love. Therefore, the more we know about others the more we are able to accomplish our goal by giving them our love.

Part V: I Gauge My Growing, Giving, and Gaining

Tracking - Strengths and Habits

Week Date Starting				mtd	14	15	16	17	18	19	20
Outgoing	Task	Dominant D	Driven - Go getter	4 /12	1	2	1	3	2	5	0 5
			Decisive								
			Definite - firm								
			Daring-bold								
			Direct-outspoken, candid								
			Delegate-designate								
			Developer-initiator								
			Leader								
			Persistent, competitive								
			Focused								
Outgoing	People	Influence I	Interactive-social, friendly								
			Informative-talkative, chatty								
			Inspiring-encourager								
			Idealist-optimistic,								
			Excited, enthused								
			Forgiving								
			Hopeful								
			Persuasive, convincing								
			Confident								
			Charismatic, charming								
Reserved	People	Steady S	Sincere, trustworthy, genuine								
			Softhearted-kind, gentle								
			Submissive-obedient								
			Supportive								
			Satisfied-content, flexible								
			Patient, relaxed, calm								
			Teamwork - cooperative								
			Loyal								
			Good listener, attentive								
Reserved	Task	Conscientious C	Cautious								
			Controlled-disciplined								
			Compliant-by the book								
			Committed								
			Considerate								
			Organized, detail oriented								
			Correct-accurate								
			Punctual								
			Careful-analytical, examining								
			Calculated-logical, rational								
Personal Tracking											
Withhold opinion											
Eat healthy											
Praise people or be quiet											
Totals											

Reader input: www.iwasborntowin.com/readerinput

Chapter 19: Tracking and Gauging

The tracking chart will help you in the following areas:

- Identify someone else's primary personality
- Familiarize yourself with individual personality strengths
- Learn specific areas where others need you
- Create new positive habits - at will

Identify another's Primary Personality

On the very left, you see the words "Outgoing or Reserved." This is the first step to determining someone's personality. If they are outgoing, start from the center of the lefthand side and go up. If they are reserved, go down. The next set of labels (step 2) identifies the orientation of each personality. You simply need to know if they are *task* or *people* oriented. These two steps allow you, through a process of elimination, to identify which primary personality a person may have.

Here is an example of determining someone else's personality. If I do not know enough about a person, I may ask, "Mary is it more natural for you to be outgoing or reserved?" Mary says she is "reserved." By looking at the chart, I know to look at the bottom half of the page and Mary is either a Steady-S or a Conscientious-C. Then I ask the next question (Step 2). "Mary, do you naturally like to work more with tasks (things) or people?" Mary says she likes to work with people. Therefore, Mary has a primary personality style of a Steady-S. This is a quick and simple way to determine a personality style. The assessment we used in the personality section of chapter 10 is better because it gets more specific. www.iwasborntowin.com/personality.

Familiarize Yourself with Individual Strengths

Each individual personality has specific strengths listed. If you look beyond your type at some of the others, you will notice that their strengths are actually your weaknesses. I want you to notice how important this is. If their strength is your weakness, then it also means your strengths will be their weaknesses. This tells us two important things:

- Other people have a need for strengths that you provide.
- Tracking allows you to pinpoint and learn the specific areas where they have those needs.

Also, by focusing on your own needs, you are actually learning the strengths of others, simultaneously. Example; a Steady-S has a strength of listening. When they overuse that strength and are too silent, it can become a weakness. There may be times when they need to speak but they stay silent. Typically, when you meet a Steady S, "talkative" could be one of their weaknesses or *area of need*. By identifying this as an area they wish to improve upon, they can mark it and start keeping track (we will cover tracking more in detail).

Next, notice which personality has the strength of "talkative" - Influence-I. Who do you think a Steady-S may want to watch, listen to, observe, and pay attention to when trying to become stronger at talking? Yes, the Influence-I. Who could a Dominant-D learn patience from - a Steady-S. There are many other dynamics to this chart. Can you see how it will help you stay focused on strengths – both yours and others? One of the greatest ways to see value in another person is focusing on their strengths. We do not need to focus on flaws, they get us nowhere. People's flaws, like claws, will always be around scratching the surface.

Learn Specific Areas Where Others Need You

As we discussed in the *"I give on the outside"* section, our purpose in life is to **give** by filling needs. You can rest assured; a person in one personality type definitely has *needs* in the other three. Remember, the needs for one personality will be the strengths of the other types and vice versa. If a person is a primary Conscientious-C with a secondary Influence-I, then we know their needs are the strengths of the Steady-S and Dominant-D. This is one reason opposite people attract to each other. Once you identify your strengths and the needs of others, you have a starting point for learning your purpose. God has given you specific strength combinations that no other person has. This also means you have specific needs no other person has. The

Chapter 19: Tracking and Gauging

more time you spend defining, perfecting, and balancing your strengths, a better *giver* you will become.

This should show you that the world really does need you! I am not suggesting, in an egotistical way, that the world cannot revolve without you. I am saying that if God made you, then he had a good reason. I am certain you have strengths that I do not have, regardless of your age, skin color, nationality, or intelligence. Personally, I am challenged daily with organization, focus, finishing what I started, listening, patience, and many other needs. These are areas of my life where I need help. As much as I love to speak and socialize, I must have other people in my life to fill in the gaps, the areas where I am not strong. All of us, to a degree, are gap-fillers. Your strengths are desired and the world has plenty of opportunities for you. Again, this can take you closer to realizing and fulfilling your purpose in life.

Creating Positive Habits

The Dutch humanist from the 1400's, Desiderius Erasmus, said *"A nail is driven out by another nail."* A habit is overcome by another habit.

This is my favorite part of the chart. It has had a profound affect on helping me create those positive habits we discussed in the last chapter. Prior to creating this chart, I tested this strategy simply by scratching tick marks on a piece of paper. The first thing I started tracking was *praise people or be quiet*. Gossip is just one of the many things in life that I had a bad habit of doing and claimed I needed to change. The results were immediate, and they were amazingly powerful. The very first month I was able to *praise people or be quiet* over 120 times! The power of this system is to track where you want to go (target), not your shortcomings or your past mistakes. Only track, view, and pay attention to the very thing you want to record into your subconscious.

At first, I would still slip and gossip. But as I continued to track, I got better and better. I now have a great habit of *praising people or being quiet*. This does not mean I am never tempted anymore. But now, most of the time, when the input comes to mind, my subconscious takes that thought captive and I avoid the gossip.

Praise people or be quiet would go on the chart at the bottom under personal tracking. The whole purpose of the personal area is to help you stay focused on behavior that is specific to you. These are behaviors that are likely *surface* behaviors rather than foundational. A surface behavior is one that is dealt with more on the surface of life. If your desire is to become smoke-free, you could track each time you choose to skip smoking a cigarette. Each time you skip smoking you are actually being *committed, responsible, loyal, etc*. You could also record tick marks in those foundational areas. Besides the personal area, you will find that most of your focus will be in the two personalities that are *not* primary or secondary to you. As we already discussed, those areas will expose most of your needs. To make this tracking chart effective and ensure you will actually do it, I suggest you circle only four to five of the foundational strengths. Those plus your specific list should be plenty for you to focus on at any given time. You can change, add, or subtract, as much as you want. This chart has the flexibility to fit your unique personality and preferences.

Week Date Starting	mtd	14	15	16	17	18	19	20
Driven - Go getter	4 12	1	2 1	3 2	3 0	3		
Decisive								
Definite - firm								
Daring-bold								

Each page covers seven days of tracking. Write the day of the week at the top of each column. When you track an action, you can simply put a tick mark in the upper portion of that particular box for that day. If you do it three times, you will have three tick marks. The bottom portion of the box is where you keep a running total for the month. If you had three ticks the first day, you would put a three in the bottom of the box. If you had two ticks the following day, you would then add those two ticks to the running total (three) for a total of five so far – month to date. Every seven days you will start a new sheet for the week. You carry your totals over for each row to the new sheet. Then you repeat the process. The whole purpose here is three-fold. One, it monitors your actions so you will be encouraged, notice progress, and keep the traction. Secondly, you are reminded to actually do the behavior (create another tick mark). Thirdly, it creates new *positive* habits. This will take a little time to get used to, but it is more than worth it. Personally, this is the best tool I have ever used for creating new positive habits.

Chapter 19: Tracking and Gauging

Summary

Points to ponder-

If we track something we stay interested.

If we stay interested we become motivated to learn, seek, explore and implement.

Old habits won't permanently leave until the time and space they're currently occupying is filled by a new activity or habit.

What would a winner do?

Track and gauge my thoughts and actions.

Summarized Outline of chapters 1-19

Winning is obtaining love.	**I *gain* from my pain**
Love must come before the wishlist.	Pain for the proper purpose is productive.
To win, I *grow* from the inside.	Winning with pain allows me to face it and appreciate the good pain.
I fill my inner fuel tank with the good, the clean, the pure, and the positive.	I respect fear and use it for winning.
I increase my self-image, daily, with self-talk and by visualizing a winner.	I align my focus to my desires instead of allowing fear to change my desires to fit my focus.
I mind my own business, don't compare myself to others, and don't gossip.	**I win more by *gauging* my growing, giving, and gaining**
I win by conceiving, believing, and achieving.	I qualify my desires and targets.
I grow inside by forgiving others.	I have a roadmap to assist me in winning. It's called a goals system.
Winning requires me to *give* on the outside.	My goals system keeps me on the winner's highway and allows me to stay focused.
By giving love I obtain love.	
I am willing to make paradigm shifts.	I track my strengths and positive habits daily.
I value the differences in people and their personality.	My tracking keeps positive actions and implementation of new habits fresh in my mind.
I understand the weaknesses and strengths of my own personality.	
I know or I am consciously seeking my purpose in life.	

I believe, with all my heart, if you will do these things throughout life, you may make mistakes, you may get knocked down, and you may even be criticized by the unwilling. But you won't go wrong because you will be doing what's right. In the event we get to meet one day, I hope to hear you say with confidence, *"I was born to win."*

As I shared in the introduction of this book, if the initial part of winning were easy, more people would be winners. It takes effort and hard work, but it is so rewarding. You deserve it, and you are fully capable. I have given you some specific plans that absolutely do work. It's important to remember - no plan will work until you do.

Make a decision, today, to start removing the excuses and accept the calling on your life. Choose, this day, to no longer accept mediocrity in any area of life. Breathe more life into any ambitions, talents, dreams, and potential that lie dormant within you. The world is a standing ovation waiting for your debut, your book, your song, your dance, and your encore. Share more of your unique and special gifts starting today!

In the next and final part of the book, I will share an experience that has allowed me to work this system most effectively. For me personally, my spiritual journey has equipped me to grow, give, gain, and gauge more effectively and joyfully than any other single factor in my life. It has taken me to levels of winning that I never even imagined. I believe your spiritual journey could do the same for you.

Part VI: A Spiritual Experience

Chapter 20
Dying a Winner

When I stand before God at the end of my life, I would hope that I would not have a single bit of talent left, and could say, "I used everything you gave me." - Erma Bombeck, American Author

Painting the Picture

Not long ago, I struggled with addictions to tobacco, alcohol, marijuana, gossip, food, pornography, sex, and co-dependency. Toward the end, I was even dabbling in cocaine, ecstasy, crack, painkillers, and muscle relaxers. Today, I am completely free from all of those addictions and poisons. The freedom came from a combination of what I've shared with you so far and what I'm about to share with you.

I was born and raised in a small farm-town just East of Tampa named Plant City, Florida. When I say small, if we stuck our head out the window we were in another town. My phone number was 26. We lived so far back in the woods we didn't get the Sunday paper until Wednesday!

There were three of us kids in my family; my step-dad was disabled, and my mother worked to pay the bills. To this day I am still amazed at how we made it on the resources we had. Fortunately, we did have lots of love, but I didn't understand the value of love then like I do now. I didn't have much as far as material possessions during my childhood. I know what it feels like to stand in line for free government cheese and powdered milk. I am very familiar with wearing second and third-hand clothes to school. I remember making up excuses to be dropped off, down the road, so my friends wouldn't see the family car. Back in those days, food stamps were distinctive coupons and it was quite embarrassing in the checkout lines at the

Part VI: A Spiritual Experience

grocery store. I know about working full-time jobs during high school and bringing the paycheck home to help cover bills. I've been embarrassed, made fun of, and ostracized because of what I possessed, or the lack of. Now please don't get me wrong; we did have plenty to eat. I know we had plenty because every time I would pass my plate for seconds, my parents would say, *"No, you've had plenty."*

My story isn't really unique, as a matter-of-fact, my story is all too common. It's common in the sense that upon entering adulthood I started chasing the wishlist in hopes of being "somebody"; rich, important, valuable – loved. As many of us do, I allowed several aspects of my childhood to paint a poor picture of me on the inside. My self-image wasn't the healthiest in the world, and I was certain the wishlist could change it. As we've already discussed about the wishlist, the harder I chased it the lower my self-image became. As long as my expectations were in the wishlist rather than love, I was unknowingly headed the wrong way. It wasn't immediate, it happened over a span of twenty years. Through many obstacles, setbacks, and heartaches on that *wrong way* street, I began to deaden the pain more and more. Eventually I would end up with numerous destructive addictions. Those behaviors ensured that my self-image went even lower.

I was miserable and lonely to say the least, but most people around me could not tell. It was an inside issue, not an outward problem. On the outside I had learned to wear a pretty good mask. I've always been a business man, enjoyed the profession of selling, and was usually looking fine from the surface. I learned early in life that if I was funny and fun to be around that I could attract people. Then as I started possessing *things*, I could attract even more people. But that motive and method of gaining importance, value, or love lead me deeper into the feelings I explained in the first sentence of this paragraph. *I was miserable and lonely to say the least.*

> "It's not the song or the dance that wears down, it's the singer and the dancer"

On December 31st, 2005 I dropped down on my knees. I was exhausted, depressed, angry, broken, and desperate. Oh, I had owned the possessions - a beautiful home, my share of luxury cars, great careers, etc. The only thing I was lacking was the only thing that ultimately matters...love. I had some love from friends and family, especially love from my wonderful daughter, with whom I am so blessed. But I didn't have enough love inside of myself to outweigh the fears and pain that controlled me. The more I used destructive addictions for coping, the more my fear and pain increased. I literally cried out and begged God to help me. At that point I started a new relationship with God that I've never regretted. Maybe this isn't the first time you've heard this song and dance. Well, it wasn't the first time I had performed it either. It's not the song or the dance that wears down, it's the singer and the dancer.

I was first introduced to God when I was eight years old. I've been going to church all my life, off and on. I had even *recommitted* in the past - a few times actually. But this last time was unusual; the difference was my perceived need for God. As I mentioned in chapter three, we are only motivated for what we think we need. Many folks are only interested in becoming smoke-free after the doctor convinces them the cigarettes will kill them. As long as we have oxygen we are not consciously motivated for it. But if the level becomes too low we want it...now! My spiritual oxygen was almost gone and I needed God. I did not need church, Christianity, or religion – I needed a spiritual relationship with God. Why God? How does God become that oxygen? I'm glad you asked, but before I answer, I want to address a common and valid concern.

False Perceptions

I realize people have a bad taste in their mouth with words like God or Jesus; so do I. That in itself is not enough of a reason to discount either of them - if they are true. Why would we have a bad taste in our mouth? The same reason we have bad tastes in our mouths about *love* or anything else in life that has significant value. Anytime something has value there will be people with wrong motives who attempt to gain from it. I've heard people slam marriage, money, kids, other people, and all sorts of valuable things. If I told you I loved you but did things opposite of love that hurt you, it still doesn't make love bad. It just means a person with wrong motives used something of good value to hurt you.

Part VI: A Spiritual Experience

God's name has probably been used more than anything else by people to scam, hurt, abuse, and destroy. Notice I said God's name has been used, I did not say God did it. Unfortunately, people use God for their own purposes, just like they use love, money, or power. All these things can be great when used with the proper motives. Too many people think God is out to get them. But they only think this because of the way people have used God, not because of God himself. Those of us who feel God know He is not out to get people. It's when we try to learn about something, through the wrong agendas of others, that we can get in trouble. If we ever think God is out to get us or wants to hurt us, it's because we've listened to someone else, not God.

I've also heard people say if God is such a good thing then why does He allow murders, rapes, and other crime. He must allow it or the whole human race would not be possible. It's the free will God gave us that even allows humanity to exist. Otherwise, we would be like many other living organisms that do not get to make choices. If we are *mad* at God it's because we were treated poorly by someone that was *mad* at someone else. As we discussed in chapter seven, bitterness is a poison. You and I can be mad at God all we want but it's the anger of the other person that really hurts us. Harboring anger against God simply prepares us to be the one who offends someone else down the road. Within twenty-four hours of writing this very paragraph, I read the following in the news and got quite the laugh.

Convict sues God for broken contract[18] - Monday July 16th, 2007

Claims deal made for divine protection from evil, 'instead he gave me to Satan' who caused murder.

A man serving a 20-year sentence for murder has been rebuffed so far in his effort to sue God for breach of contract by failing to protect him from evil and turning him over to Satan who encouraged him to kill.

Pavel Mircea, 40, filed his lawsuit in the western Romanian town of Timisoara, charging God with failure to fulfill an agreement Micera alleged was made at his baptism. "He was supposed to protect me from all evils and instead he gave me to Satan who encouraged me to kill," he charged. In the lawsuit, Mircea listed "God, resident in heaven, represented in Romania by the Orthodox church" as the defendant, according to the Romanian daily Evenimentul Zilei.

Chapter 20: Dying a Winner

God's alleged dereliction, according to Mircea, included fraud, breach of trust, abuse of a position of authority, and misappropriation of goods – all crimes, the plaintiff noted, under the Romanian criminal code. Mircea said that God had accepted his prayers and sacrificial offerings without providing any services in return. Thus far, Mircea is not getting an answer to his prayer to the court for relief, either.

I assume you've heard it said before – facts are stranger than fiction. This is a classic case of someone not taking responsibility for their own actions and attempting to blame God. While it was for his own selfish motive, he did at least acknowledge the existence of God.

I'm always intrigued by those who claim there is not a God simply because they've never felt or known Him. They use the perceived absence of something in their own life to prove it doesn't exist. That's almost like me saying there's no cancer because I've never experienced it. Sure, I've heard other people say they have it and even witnessed the effects of it. But since I've never seen it, had it, or felt it I don't believe in it.

This ultimately leads back to people putting a value on God based on experiences by other people. If I focused on all the people who have been hurt or killed because of driving in a car, I doubt I would ever get in a vehicle again. The car isn't the problem; it's the people using the cars. God will never *ever* be the problem, only the solution. Once I realized this, the doors of freedom opened wide.

The Oxygen of Life

Here's how God became the oxygen I needed. You see, God **is** love. God is the ultimate of the ultimate love. He is the *mack-daddy* of love! When you and I feel love, regardless of where it comes from, we are feeling....God! I want to emphasize again, I'm not talking about sex, or making love, or being in love, or romance, or loving a car. Many of those things, when abused, come with fear and pain. I'm talking about the love we discussed in chapter two - true love. Not only is God love, He is perfect love, pure, zero fear - the *only* source of unconditional love that you and I can ever possibly know. Proverbs says we all desire unfailing love[19]. If you could have this source available to you, day and night, it's easy to admit - it's not a bad deal! You may be thinking, *"How do you know this James? I've heard so many different opinions. It doesn't really make sense; it's confusing and seems illogical."*

Faith or Facts

I agree - it is very confusing and difficult to understand. I'm even confused about simpler things - like how radio waves travel through the air and allow me to hear a broadcast from New York to Florida immediately, but I tune in. I'm confused at how electricity works, how it powers a light bulb, and how light gives illumination - but I still use them. I do not have to understand something in order for it to work. This is the most important thing I have to remember about God. If He was easy enough for my little mind to grasp and understand completely, I can assure you, he would not be the God that He is.

Larry King, one of the best interviewers on the planet, summed it up as well as I've ever heard. He was asked recently, by Anderson Cooper from CNN, if he believed in God. He simply said that he doesn't really know. He said he is fascinated by both arguments (God vs. no God) but ultimately his *intellect* gets in the way. I believe he speaks for many of us. But just as we enjoy love, we can also enjoy God. Both are difficult to wrap your mind around, and yet both of them will fill your heart with joy that's indescribable.

God is not something to be understood with our head, He is something and someone to be experienced and obtained within our heart. The reason we believe in the wind is because we are able to feel it and see the proof it exists. This is why I know God is the best love in the world - I feel him daily! I can never introduce you to God. I can never let you meet the God I experience, but you can experience and obtain God in *your* own heart. Then and only then can you understand what I am saying.

Having a relationship with God takes faith, *and then* facts are revealed. You *will* feel Him. Faith is the very essence of things not seen or understood. If facts revealed faith, there would be no need for faith. Faith, on the other hand, will reveal the facts. Through faith you can experience a real knowledge of God and obtain the real love of

God; but it takes faith first. This is an area where Larry King and others say they have the difficulty when trying to overcome the logics. Amazingly, when you finally have the faith to give God a chance, He will make himself known to you in a way that will become very factual to you. I'm not suggesting that you give your family, your friend, or your spouse a chance – give God a chance!

Suppose what I am saying is just something I conjured up in my mind, a figment of my imagination. For the sake of conversation, suppose that humans have this incredible ability to dream up what I am sharing with you. Then ask yourself this please, "Where does the ability to dream up such a thing come from? What or where is the energy that creates this?" The absence of something doesn't always prove it does not exist, it simply proves it's not seen, perceived, felt, or noticed – thus far. This is why it all boils down to faith, which in turn, will provide us with proper knowledge.

The Owner's Manual

In order to have proper expectations about anything it helps if we have proper knowledge. I just bought a new cell phone. It does everything but shine my shoes - internet, video, camera, dictator, mp3 player, email, and phone. I've only read small parts of the owner's manual so far. I get frustrated with the phone sometimes because it does not do what I am expecting it to do. Will you re-read what I just said? *I get frustrated with the phone because it doesn't do what I expect it to do.* Wouldn't my expectations be proper or more realistic if I would read more of the owner's manual? Then I would know what I *should* be expecting. In all fairness, shouldn't I be getting frustrated with, uhm, *me?*

Most of us set expectations on God without knowing all the details. We take the words of others without reading the owner's manual. I do not set expectations on God unless the Bible (God's owners manual) tells me to. And if I do set expectations without reading the manual, I can only blame me, not God. You may ask how anyone knows the Bible is true. That's a very valid question. Ultimately it boils down to faith, and personally I believe the whole Bible - from Genesis to maps! But here are a few facts you may find interesting.

Fact 1 – The Bible changes the heart of humans. You experience emotions that are inexplicable as a result of reading the Bible. Have you ever read it? How often do you read it? I'm not asking how often you've listened to someone else talk about it. Imagine if you heard that God was coming to town; that He would be here for a week and anyone who wanted could come meet and learn about Him, one-on-one. Would you get opinions from others or would you go check Him out for yourself? The Bible is God speaking directly to you.

Fact 2 – No one has ever proven the Bible to be false, ever. Many of those who try become great promoters of God. The Bible took 1,600 years to complete; it consists of 66 different books written by over thirty different authors. They were in different places and spoke different languages, yet it fits together just like a jigsaw puzzle. Divine inspiration is what enables such odds to take place. Is it mathematically possible that it could happen without God? Maybe, but with odds like that, I'll put my faith in God.

Fact 3 – The Bible is the all-time best selling book in history, by a long shot. Over sixty-six billion have been sold! It was outlawed from being read in schools in the U.S. and still sells more than any other book, year in and year out. People are interested in what it has to say - we really do want love. Psalm 33:18 says, "But the eyes of the Lord are on those who fear [*respect*] Him, on those whose hope is in His unfailing love" (emphasis added by me). Proverbs 19:22 says, "What a man desires is unfailing love." If you have ever wanted a source that delivers perfect truth, the Bible is it. Do you know of any other source that claims that? People cannot; other books cannot; only God's Word.

Fact 4 – The Bible commands respect like no other book. Take it to a restaurant, to school, to the movies. It gets attention, it gets noticed. God's spirit is alive and well, and He is available for us, day or night, in abundance.

God created you with a desire to love him[20]. Genesis says God created us in his image to have a love relationship with him. God loves us no matter what, unconditionally. Does this mean he loves thieves, robbers, murderers, everyone? Absolutely! He hates their behavior (sin), but he loves them. When I really grasped the idea that God loves me for me, no other reason, I got excited. I mean, think about it;

Chapter 20: Dying a Winner

the perfect source of love, which is my ultimate human desire, loves me unconditionally. Are you kidding me? I was happier than fire ants on pizza!

If you are open enough to check it out for yourself, you will at least be able to determine, based on your own opinion, if God has a value to offer you. Until we notice a value in God, we will not believe we have a need for him. Until we have a need for Him, we will not be motivated to seek Him.

Eternal Love

Here are two great reasons why one might desire to have a direct relationship with God – unfiltered love and eternal love.

Unfiltered love means you experience it directly from God to you. It does not filter through any other living entity, such as a person or animal. It is God's spirit of perfect love, unflawed love, and unconditional love living within you[21]. Any love that you and I receive through others is dependent upon their willingness to give it or allow it to flow through them, it is filtered[22] - conditioned. This is because God does not force anyone to love, therefore, it's through free will and choice. Once connected directly to God, His love bypasses any kind of filters or conditions. I don't know about you, but I know a good deal when I see it.

Eternal love is the ultimate "winning" because, in addition to being perfect and unfiltered, He never ends - ever. In a world with so many letdowns, it is awesome to know we can have a perfect source that is eternal and will never let us down. In the Bible, from the book of Hebrews[23], God tells us he will never leave us or forsake us. I know of no other source that can make such a promise *and* keep it.

The Bible teaches that we all have a spirit that never ends. Even though our physical body dies, our spirit lives forever. By *our choice*, we have the option to determine where we spend eternity. We can spend eternity with zero love, total separation of love, otherwise known as hell. I don't know about you but I have experienced a taste of hell on earth, I certainly have no desire to spend eternity in such a miserable condition.

On the other hand, we have the choice of spending eternity with perfect love, God, starting now. Additionally, we become perfect upon entering Heaven. Not only do we get to spend eternity with the perfect source of love in God, we also get to spend it with others we currently love. I cannot accurately or justly explain the peace and joy I have because I know I get to spend eternity with my family and many of my friends who've also chosen this route. Again, I know a pretty good deal when I see one. Putting it quite simple, we will be dead a whole lot longer than we will be alive. Knowing our destiny and security on the other side of eternity is quite helpful and hopeful.

God, the perfect love Himself, *wants* a relationship with you and me. He wants it so badly that he sent his son Jesus to die on the cross (John 3:16, NIV). You might ask why it happened that way. Because God is perfect love and humans are imperfect; we have sin in our blood (Romans 3:23, NIV). God could not possibly be perfect if He mixed directly with sin. It would be like dropping an ounce of oil into a gallon of milk. Even the slightest drop and the milk would no longer be pure. This is why Jesus shed His blood and covered all of our sins - past, present, and future. He did it so that you and I, through Jesus, could have a relationship with God. That's how awesome this source of love is that I'm sharing with you.

No matter what kind of shape we are currently in or what our lifestyle is, God wants to meet us just the way we are. It doesn't matter if you're struggling with addictions, relationship issues, job issues, criminal issues, or any other issues. Nor does it necessarily mean you will immediately stop struggling. It simply means you will now have the absolute best counselor and assistant that one could ever have in life. It also means you have eternal love after this life. This relationship ends any question of what happens after death.

Imagine God is a gated private community (we will call it *God's Kingdom*) one that's holy and perfect and allows no sin inside. Jesus is at the entrance gate. When we want to enter we must go through Him because He is the sponge of our sins. He is the one who absorbed them, and we must allow Him to wash away our sins so we can enter *God's Kingdom,* sin-free. When we do this, we then have an eternal relationship with God. God's Spirit lives in our heart forever and allows us to have a perfect line of communication with Him. I mean a toll-free hotline, no dropped calls, and no bad signals - a perfect connection. It does not make us perfect, but it allows a perfect connection with the perfect One, and the ability to connect day or night.

Eternal Security

Here's the conclusion of Tony Dungy's speech (from chapter 14 – *Why Does God Allow Pain in our Life*) that was given just after his son, James, committed suicide.

I got a letter from a girl in our church that had grown up with James, and she said, "You know, we've been going to the same church in Tampa for all these years. I sat there in church every Sunday but never really knowing if there was a God or not. I came to the funeral because I knew James. When I saw what happened at the funeral, and your family and the celebration and how it was handled, that was the first time I realized there has to be a God. I accepted Christ into my life, and my life's been different since that day." And that was an awesome blessing.

All those things have kind of made me realize what God's love is all about. But here, the biggest part of that, I know in my heart that James' death has affected many people and benefited many people. And that makes me feel better, but I also know this; if God had had a conversation with me and said, "I can help some people see; I can heal some relationships; I can save some people's lives; I can give some people eternal life, but I have to take your son to do it, you make the choice." I know how I would have answered that. I would have said, "No, I'm sorry. As great as all that is, I don't want to do that." And that's the awesome thing about God. He had that choice, and He said, "Yes, I'm going to do it," 2,000 years ago with His Son, Jesus, on the cross. And because He said yes, because He made the choice that I wouldn't make as a parent, that's paved the way for us to come back into relationship with Him. That's paved the way for us to see changed lives like Curtis'. That's let us know with certainty that we can live in heaven. That's the benefit I got by accepting Christ into my heart; that's the benefit James got.

I went back to work one week after my son died. I had a lot of media people; a lot of sportswriters, a lot of fans ask me, "How could you get back to work so quick after something like that? How have you recovered so quickly?" I'm not totally recovered, I don't know if I ever will be. It's still very, very painful. But I was able to come back because of something one of my good Christian friends said to me after the funeral. He said this, "You know, James accepted Christ into his heart, so you know he's in heaven, right?" I said, "Right, I know that." "So with all you know about heaven, if you had the power to bring him back right now, would you?" When I thought about that, I said, "No, I wouldn't. I would not want him back with what I know about heaven." That's what helped me through the grieving process because of Christ's Spirit in me. I had that confidence that James is there at peace with the Lord, and I have the peace of mind in the midst of something that's very, very painful. That's my prayer today, that everyone in this room would know that same thing. "Why does God allow pain in our life?" Dungy asked in his emotionally charged speech. "Because we are loved by God and the pain allows us to head back to our Father."

Does all of this take faith? Yes. Does it take submission, humility, and trust? Yes. If I'm wrong, all you have to lose is a little pride, or perhaps a little letdown. If I'm right, you have eternity to be concerned about. Most of us make more leaps of faith every day when we drive in traffic. We believe the other drivers will stay in their lane. When our traffic light is green we believe the lights adjacent to us are red. It takes a whole lot more faith to get married than it does to meet God. We have faith every day that the food we eat is clean and not tainted - we put a lot of faith in others.

Although millions have established a relationship with God, I have never met one person who regretted it, not one. How's that for statistics? If you are willing to do what you can do in life, God is willing to do what you can't do. Would you like to trust Him today? Do you want to take winning to a whole other level?

The Bible says in Romans 10:9(NIV) that if you confess with your mouth that Jesus is Lord and believe in your heart that God raised Him from the dead, then you will be saved. Saved means eternal security with perfect love that we have been discussing. This is not just lip service, this is a belief– it is having faith. But it is not difficult either. Notice it said *believe* not logically understand. It is a belief deep within your heart; it is a request to God for eternal love and salvation.

Nowhere in the Bible does it say we have to stop smoking, or stop drinking alcohol, get out of prison, or stop anything. It says we must believe in our heart. If we waited until we stopped everything in our life that is labeled as *bad*, we would never get to meet God. You don't wait until you're well to go see the doctor. You go to the doctor in order to get well. God is the master physician who is waiting for you to come to Him, just as you are. The thief on the cross, hanging next to Jesus, had a rough past but he made a choice that gave him a perfect future. At the lowest time of his life, he made a choice for Jesus. You also have a choice.

If you want to begin a personal relationship with God right now and have eternal salvation, please say this prayer from your heart. *God I recognize Jesus as Lord and request that my sins be covered by His blood. God, I believe in my heart that You raised Jesus from the dead. Will you please save me and give me eternal love? Thank you for saving me God.*

If you just said that prayer **from your heart**, congratulations! You have just joined the family of perfect love. The Bible also tells us that nothing can ever separate us from the love of God[24]. What other source can make these types of promises and back them up? As you continue your new journey and growth towards learning and knowing God better, you will understand and feel more of His perfect love. It's unlike anything I can adequately describe.

The Power of Perfect Love

I've made some terrible choices in life and went down some bad roads. There are things in my life that are far from perfect, but there's a love in my life that is absolutely perfect. I've made choices in my life that have hurt me and others tremendously. But there's a love in my life that heals those that hurt. God's love is the real deal, period.

I'm not a Bible scholar or theologian, but I would like to point out a most interesting thought for you to ponder. After describing *love* in the Bible, from the book of Corinthians, the Apostle Paul goes on to say, *"And these three things remain; faith, hope, and love, but the greatest of these is love."* I believe most of us understand the power of faith and hope. We realize how faith and hope shape our thoughts, our actions, our past, and certainly our future. As powerful as both of them are, Paul tells us that love is greater. Think about this for a moment. When we finally meet with the One and only perfect source of love, face–to-face, faith and hope will no longer be needed! Faith and hope, as powerful as both are have no more value when finally in the presence of perfect love because there will be nothing else to have faith or hope for. It will be the only sure time of our existence when we can literally know and say, *"I've arrived"* or *"I won!"* No wonder it's called heaven[25]. This baffles my mind; the thought of being in the personal presence of pure love, of God Himself, is so powerful. I visualize, in my mind's eye, it going like this: *"Hi, this is perfect love, come on in. Go ahead and leave any faith or hope you have at the door. They are no longer required, ever."* Wow!

Until that wonderful time comes, I highly encourage you to take full advantage of your current faith, hope, and love. We are flawed people in a flawed world on a flawed journey looking for perfection. A wonderful source to help you and me on this journey is consistently reading God's words – the Bible (**basic instructions for the best living on earth**). You may want to start in the New Testament - the book of John. God will talk to you personally through the Bible. You will feel Him. He will encourage you, love you, and help you grow. If you already have this awesome relationship; it is my prayer that you are taking full advantage of it by choosing to consistently pursue more of God.

Summary

Points to ponder –

God is the perfect source of true love.

God wanted a loving relationship with you so bad that He sent His son Jesus to die for you.

God loves you just the way you are.

Love is stronger than both faith and hope.

What would a winner do?

Grow as close to God as possible.

Read my Bible and pray often.

Chapter 20: Dying a Winner

In closing, perhaps you have thought, "James, are you suggesting that I read the Bible every day? Are you suggesting that I do the 'self-talk' card, the tracking, and the goals system every day? Is all of this growing, giving, gaining, and gauging stuff necessary *every* day?" Those are great questions and worthy of addressing. I do not think it is necessary to take these actions every day. You should only do them on the days you want to win more. Just like eating or bathing, neither is required every day but life seems to be a little better when we do them.

You really were born to win. You can choose to do so, often. Life needs more winners. Are you up for the challenge to win more? Think it, say it, believe it, & **live** it *"I was born to win!"*

Knock'em alive!

James A. Smith

Acknowledgements

I must first thank one of my favorite hero's, Zig Ziglar, for his constant encouragement. Through the many years of hearing him tell me *I was born to win,* combined with the grace of my Lord, I am now living the life of a winner. The *Born to Win* workshops helped change my life and many around me as well. The workshops ignited the spark that motivated me to change careers and also write this book. I would like to thank those on the Ziglar team who added so much to the workshops - Michael McGowan, Tom Ziglar, Krish Dhanam, Laurie Magers, John Foppe, Jean Ziglar (Zig's wife whom he lovingly calls *The Redhead*), Amy Jones, Katherine Lemons, and Bryan Flanagan. I have especially appreciated all of the insight, wisdom, and availability whenever I have called upon Michael McGowan and Bryan Flanagan.

My friend, Velvet Torres, must be given credit for prompting me to start this project when I did. Her willingness to help me in the areas where I am weak enabled me to start writing much earlier than anticipated. She was also very helpful with editing.

I want to thank the others who took part in the editing; John Gregory, MariLynn Polachek, and Amy Merrill. Amy was especially helpful for her extra ideas and willingness to challenge me.

I want to thank Gary Salyers and Chip Powell for your concentrated efforts in reviewing this book in such a quick manner. Additionally, I thank Dr. Tim Passmore, Eric Freeman, Banks Corl, Patrick Tomasi, Tammy McDermid, Pastor Kevin M. Wynne, Terry Miller, Michael Schwambach, Billy Tullos, Mike Holman Sr., Pastor Phil Grimes, Duane Lee, Bill Arthur, Virna Maldonado, Randy and Debbie Lipp (and family), Anthony and Rhonda Barbacane, my brother Andy "Drew" Smith, Mike and MariLynn Polachek, Kelley McDermid, and Steve Smith for your reviews, feedback, or willingness to allow me to bounce ideas back and forth with you.

I also want to thank my friends in the Forum Singles group at Woodland Community Church for your continued support and encouragement.

Michael Schwambach has helped me from the beginning with ideas, concepts, and the delivery of content. His high integrity and love for the Lord has proven to be a very valuable part of this book. I appreciate the friendship we have created.

Dr. David Anderson, pastor of Faith Baptist Church in Sarasota, Florida gives me consistent content and ideas through his extraordinary ability to perceive and deliver topics in his newsletters.

Cassandra Smith, "Boogie," my beautiful daughter, has played a significant role in helping with ideas and giving me feedback throughout this book. I also want to thank my ex-wife, Nina Smith, who was flexible (as always) with our visitation schedule as I attempted to meet certain deadlines while writing.

I appreciate the help of Mark Spatz and Sara Lipp for their assistance in creating the cover. And I want to thank Lee Ann Martin for her creation of the book cover's logo.

I want to acknowledge the media sources which helped me with my research and general content. My local papers, *The Herald Tribune* and *The Bradenton Herald* are constant sources. *USA Today*, *Psychology Today*, and *The New York Times* have also been valuable resources.

Footnotes/References

[1] http://www.hhmi.org/about/
[2] *Psychology Today*. Title – The Power of Love. Publication – *Psyched For Success*. Publication date – December 1, 2002 by Ellen McGrath.
[3] *Family* meaning Paul's church family. 1 Corinthians Chapter 13 - NIV
[4] Song of Solomon 8:6 and 7 – NLV
[5] http://www.secretservice.gov/whoweare.shtml
[6] 1 John 4:18 NIV
[7] This story is from a commodities guru named Ken Roberts who allegedly took the driving course.
[8] *You are what You Think*, Dr David Stoop, published by Spire, page 30
[9] http://abcnews.go.com/2020/story?id=2685717&page=1
[10] Published by Prometheus Nemesis Book Company, copyright 1998
[11] Charles C Finn claims to have written this passage in 1966 and also claims he never had it copyrighted. http://www.poetrybycharlescfinn.com/stories.html
[12] http://www.amw.com/about_amw/john_walsh.cfm
[13] Published in *Sports Illustrated* in 2005, titled as Strongest Dad in the World
[14] Shared by James Robison on his TV Show, *Life Today*, broadcasted 11.19.07
[15] Information was found at www.madd.org
[16] 2 Timothy 1:7 King James Version
[17] http://en.wikipedia.org/wiki/Space_Shuttle_external_tank
[18] http://www.worldnetdaily.com/news/article.asp?ARTICLE_ID=56680
[19] Proverbs 19:22(NIV)
[20] Proverbs 19:22(NIV), 1 John 4:16(NIV),1 John 4:12(NIV), Hebrews 13:5(NIV)
[21] 1 John 4:16(NIV)
[22] 1 John 4:12(NIV)
[23] Hebrews 13:5(NIV)
[24] Romans 8:39(NIV)
[25] 1 Corinthians 2:9(NIV)